CADENCES
OF HOME

CADENCES OF HOME

Preaching among Exiles

Walter Brueggemann

Westminster John Knox Press
Louisville, Kentucky

Most scripture quotations are from the New Revised Standard Version
of the Bible, copyright © 1989 by the Division of Christian Education
of the National Council of the Churches of Christ in the U.S.A.,
and used by permission.
Some scripture quotations are the author's own translations.

Book design by Jennifer K. Cox
Cover design by Kevin Darst

First edition
Published by Westminster John Knox Press
Louisville, Kentucky

This book is printed on acid-free paper that meets the
American National Standards Institute Z39.48 standard. ∞

PRINTED IN THE UNITED STATES OF AMERICA
02 03 04 05 06 — 10 9 8 7 6 5

Library of Congress Cataloging-in-Publication Data

Brueggemann, Walter.
    Cadences of home : preaching among exiles / Walter Brueggemann.—1st ed.
        p.   cm.
    Includes bibliographical references and index.
    ISBN 0-664-25749-6 (alk. paper)
    1. Preaching.   2. United States—Civilization—20th century.   3. United States—Moral
conditions.   I. Title.
BV4211.2.B745   1997
251'.00973—dc21   97–18835

For
HALE SCHROER

Contents

Preface

I am glad to share these thoughts with my fellow preachers and with those who support and heed my fellow preachers. I am aware that preaching—like every dimension of pastoral ministry—now becomes much more risky and demanding than it has been in any recent memory. It is my thought that if preachers and listeners might together "catch up" to our profoundly changed social circumstance, we might proceed with a different set of presuppositions and very different urgencies. Such a "catch up" could not only alleviate pressure but generate a new common gladness among us.

I am not at all sure I have got the notion of "exile" exactly right for our time and place and circumstance, for it is easy to say—against the image of exile—that the church among us is not that radically disestablished. At best, "exile" is a metaphor that, as Sallie McFague reminds us, always *is* and *is not*. Nonetheless, I believe that the metaphor can be generative and energizing for our common work, even if it does not admit of precision, for metaphors do not aim at precision.

Just as I was finishing this book, I discovered Frederick Buechner's new book, *The Longing for Home: Recollections and Reflections* (San Francisco: HarperSanFrancisco, 1996). As always Buechner's exquisite articulation makes things not only clear but also thick. Particularly in chapters 1, 6, and 8, Buechner works the themes of exile and homecoming:

> We carry inside us a *vision* of wholeness that we sense is our true home and that beckons us (110).
>
> Joy is home, and I believe that the tears that came to our eyes were more than anything else homesick tears (128).
>
> Woe to us indeed if we forget the homeless ones who have no vote, no power, nobody to lobby for them, and who might as well have no faces even, the way we try to avoid the troubling sight of them in the streets of the cities where they roam like stray cats. And

as we listen each night to the news of what happened in our lives that day, woe to us if we forget our own homelessness (104).

To be homeless the way people like you and me are apt to be homeless is to have homes all over the place but not to be really at home in any of them. To be really at home is to be really at peace, and our lives are so intricately interwoven that there can be no real peace for any of us until there is peace for all of us (140).

Buechner is ever the poet who imagines before us. But since he and I have shared the same defining teacher, it does not surprise me that he also will characteristically show his poetic voice to have ethical starch, as it always must for Israel's best vision.

This book represents a heavy-duty rethinking for myself of the art and act of preaching. I have carried on this reflection in the haunting company of my cherished preaching teachers. First among them was my father, August Brueggemann, who proceeded with uncommon courage in preaching, but who would be glad to have me move beyond the ways he did it. My two preaching teachers in seminary, Frederick W. Schroeder and Ernest F. Nolte, were caustic and severe in criticism, as well as loomingly tall. Now I see, belatedly, that their ready criticism and seeming lack of humor or grace about our learning to preach was a measure of their sense of urgency. In the end it is that sense of urgency that is their primary bequest to me and my comrades from those days, urgency that I hope is duly voiced in these pages. My debts to them are very great, even as I claim their permission to unlearn much of their way as an act of fidelity.

I am grateful to my colleagues, Charles Campbell and Stan Saunders, for their good colleagueship in reading and greatly strengthening (by correction) parts of this book. To Tempie Alexander, yet one more time, a word of thanks for uncommon diligence, unending patience, and unrivaled graciousness. In addition, I am grateful to Tim Simpson who has handled editorial chores within the manuscript.

I am pleased to dedicate this book to my long-time friend and colleague, Hale Schroer. He embodies those passions, skills, and sensitivities I most prize in preaching. He has gone on, moreover, to think long and well about the liturgical context of preaching. I have learned much from him, not least, to continue to learn.

Acknowledgments

The following chapters in *Cadences of Home* first appeared in the following publications and are reprinted with permission.

Chapter 1. "Preaching to Exiles," *Journal for Preachers* 16 (Pentecost, 1993):3–15.

Chapter 2. "Cadences Which Redescribe: Speech Among Exiles," *Journal for Preachers* 17 (Easter 1994):10–17.

Chapter 3. "Preaching as Reimagination," *Theology Today* 52 (1995):313–29.

Chapter 7. "Rethinking 'Church Models' through Scripture," *Theology Today* 48 (1991):128–38.

Chapter 8. "Disciplines of Readiness," *Occasional Paper No. 1*, Theology and Worship Unit, Presbyterian Church (U.S.A.), 1989.

1

Preaching to Exiles

I have elsewhere proposed that the Old Testament experience of and reflection upon exile is a helpful *metaphor* for understanding our current faith situation in the U.S. church, and a *model* for pondering new forms of ecclesiology.[1] (Jack Stotts in parallel fashion has suggested that the "period of the Judges" might be a more useful metaphor.[2] Stotts's suggestion has considerable merit, but because we are speaking of metaphors, these suggestions are not mutually exclusive.) The usefulness of a metaphor for rereading our own context is that it is not claimed to be a one-on-one match to "reality," as though the metaphor of "exile" actually *describes* our situation. Rather a metaphor proceeds by having only an odd, playful, and ill-fitting match to its reality, the purpose of which is to illuminate and evoke dimensions of reality which will otherwise go unnoticed and therefore unexperienced.[3]

The Metaphor of Exile

Utilization of the metaphor of "exile" for the situation of the church in the United States is not easy or obvious, and for some not compelling. I suggest the metaphor is more difficult in the South, where establishment Christianity may still be perceived as "alive and well." For those who perceive it so, what follows likely will not be useful or persuasive. My conviction, however, is that even midst such a positive perception of old religious-cultural realities, there is indeed a growing uneasiness about the sustenance of old patterns of faith and life. That uneasiness may be signaled by anxiety about "church growth," and about increasingly problematic denominational budgets.[4]

I wish, however, to tilt the metaphor of exile in a very different direction, one not occupied with issues of institutional well-being or quantitative measure, but with the experienced anxiety of "deported" people. My concern is not institutional, but pastoral. The exiled Jews of the Old Testament were of course geographically displaced. More than that, however, the exiles experienced a loss of the structured, reliable world which gave them meaning and coherence, and they found themselves in a context where their most treasured and trusted symbols of faith were mocked, trivialized, or dismissed.[5] Exile is not primally geographical, but it is social, moral, and cultural.[6]

I believe that this sense of (1) *loss of a structured, reliable "world"* where (2) *treasured symbols of meaning are mocked and dismissed* is a pertinent point of contact between those ancient texts and our situation. On the one hand, I suggest an *evangelical dimension* to exile in our social context.[7] That is, serious, reflective Christians find themselves increasingly at odds with the dominant values of consumer capitalism and its supportive military patriotism; there is no easy or obvious way to hold together core faith claims and the social realities around us. Reflective Christians are increasingly "resident aliens" (even if one does not accept all of the ethical, ecclesiological extrapolations of Stanley Hauerwas and William H. Willimon).[8] If it be insisted that church members are still in places of social power and influence, I suggest that such Christians only need to act and speak out of any serious conviction concerning the public claims of the gospel, and it becomes promptly evident that we are outsiders to the flow of power. I propose that pastors and parishioners together may usefully take into account this changed social reality of the marginalization of faith, a marginalization perhaps felt most strongly by young people.[9]

On the other hand, I suggest a *cultural dimension* to exile that is more "American" than Christian, but no less germane to the pastoral task. The "homeland" in which all of us have grown up has been defined and dominated by white, male, Western assumptions which were, at the same time, imposed and also willingly embraced. Exile comes as those values and modes of authority are being effectively and progressively diminished. That diminishment is a source of deep displacement for many, even though for others who are not male and white, it is a moment of emancipation. The deepness of the displacement is indicated, I imagine, by the reactive assault on so-called political correctness, by ugly humor, and by demonizing new modes of power.[10] For all these quite visible resistances to the new, however, we are now required to live in a new situation that for many feels like less than "home." In such a context, folk need pastoral help in relinquishing a "home" that is gone, and in entering a new "dangerous" place that we sense as deeply alien.

I suggest that the "exile" (as metaphor) is a rich resource for fresh discernment, even though a *Christian exile* in a secular culture, and a *cultural exile* with the loss of conventional hegemony are very different. In fact, the two "exiles" (evangelical and "American") arise from the fact that establishment Christianity and establishment culture have been in a close and no longer sustainable alliance. This quite concrete double focus on "exile" is a practical manifestation of what Martin Buber has called "an epoch of homelessness," brought on by the intellectual revolution around the figures of John Locke, Thomas Hobbes, and René Descartes, wherein old certitudes have been lost.[11] My interest is not in a long-term philosophical question, but in the quite specific experience of the present church. I believe that this deep sense of displacement touches us all— liberal and conservative—in personal and public ways. For that reason, the preacher must take into account the place where the faithful church must now live.

Faith in Exile

I propose that in our preaching and more general practice of ministry, we ponder the interface of our *circumstance of exile* (to the extent that this is an appropriate metaphor) and *scriptural resources* that grew from and address the faith crisis of exile. (Note well that this suggested interface entails refocusing our attention, energy, and self-perception. In times when the church could assume its own "establishment," it may have been proper to use prophetic texts to address "kings." But a new circumstance suggests a very different posture for preaching and pastoral authority, now as an exile addressing exiles, in which displacement, failed hopes, anger, wistful sadness, and helplessness permeate our sense of self, sense of community, and sense of future.)

The most remarkable observation one can make about this interface of *exilic circumstance* and *scriptural resources* is this: Exile did not lead Jews in the Old Testament to abandon faith or to settle for abdicating despair, nor to retreat to privatistic religion. On the contrary, exile evoked the most brilliant literature and the most daring theological articulation in the Old Testament. There is indeed something characteristically and deeply Jewish about such a buoyant response to trouble, a response that in Christian parlance can only be termed "evangelical," that is, grounded in a sense and sureness of *news* about God that circumstance cannot undermine or negate. That "news," which generates buoyant theological imagination in ancient Israel, is so "hard core" that it is prerational and does not submit to the "data" of historical circumstance. I suggest this is a time when preachers are "liberated" to assert that hard-core, prerational buoyance in a church too much in the grip of the defeatist sensibility of our evident cultural collapse.

For many preachers, this assertion will require considerations of texts and families of texts that were not studied in seminary. They were not studied in seminary precisely because "exile" seemed remote from us, something at the most that belonged to "late Judaism."[12] As a guide into these "new" texts, I suggest three useful resources: (1) Peter Ackroyd, *Exile and Restoration*, the classic English text on the subject, providing the "meat and potatoes" of historical criticism;[13] (2) Ralph W. Klein, *Israel in Exile*, a more accessible book that exhibits theological, pastoral sensitivity;[14] and (3) Daniel L. Smith, *The Religion of the Landless*, a daring socio-historical study that is most suggestive for seeing into the visceral elements of the circumstance, literature, and faith of the ancient exiles.[15]

While the subject of faith in exile is exceedingly rich, here I suggest six interfaces of the *circumstance of exile* and *scriptural resources*:[16]

1. Exiles must grieve their loss and express their resentful sadness about what was and now is not and will never again be. In our culture, we must be honest about the waning of our "great days" of world domination (before the rise of the Japanese economy), and all of the awkward economic complications that we experience in quite personal and immediate ways. In the church, we may be honest about the loss of our "great days" when our churches and their pastors, and even our demoninations, were forces for reckoning as they are not now. I suggest that congregations must be, in intentional ways, *communities of honest sadness*, naming the losses. We might be Jews on "the ninth of Av," when every year Jews celebrate and grieve the destruction of Jerusalem in 587 B.C.E., a destruction that persists for Jews in paradigmatic ways.[17] This community of sadness has as its work the countering of the "culture of denial" which continues to imagine that it is as it was, even when our experience tells otherwise.

The obvious place for scriptural resources for such work is in the book of Lamentations, the text used by Jews for that holy day of grieving on the Ninth of Av. Because the text is "canon," it intends to be used for many sadnesses of a communal kind, well beyond the concrete loss of Jerusalem. In the book of Lamentations, I suggest three motifs among many that warrant attention: (a) The collection of poems begins with a sustained and terrible negativity: "no resting place" (1:3), "no pasture" (1:6), "no one to help" (1:7), "none to comfort" (1:9, 16, 17, 21; 2:13), "no rest" (2:18). The poem is candid and preoccupied about loss. (b) The poetic collection ends with a pathos-filled statement (which may be a dependent clause as in NRSV, or a question as in RSV). In either case, the final statement is preceded in verse 20 with a haunting question to which Israel does not know the answer, a question about being "forgotten" and "abandoned" by God. (c) In 3:18–23, we witness the characteristically poignant Jewish ne-gotiation between sadness and hope. Verse 18 asserts that hope is gone. In verse 21, hope reappears, because in verses 22–23, Israel voices its three great terms of buoyancy, "steadfast love, mercy, faithfulness." These words do not here triumph, but they hover in the very midst of Israel's sadness, and refuse to be pushed out of the artistic discernment of the Jews. Because the sadness is fully voiced, one can see the community begin to move in its buoyancy, but not too soon. This practice of *buoyance through sadness* is one many pastors know about in situations of "bereavement." We have, however, not seen that the category of "bereavement" operates communally as well, concerning the loss of our "great days," as a superpower with an economy to match, or as a church that now tends to be a "has been."

The sadness of Jews in exile can of course grow much more shrill. It is then not a far move from lament to rage, classically expressed in Psalm 137. The psalm is of course an embarrassment to us, because of its "lethal" ending. And yet every pastor knows about folk with exactly such rage, and for exactly the same reasons. We seethe, as did they, over unfair losses that leave us displaced and orphaned. With such texts, the church need not engage in pious cover-up or false assurance. This psalm in its rage is an act of "catching up" with new reality. If Zion's songs are to be sung, it will be a long, long way from all old "Zions." The psalmist is beginning to engage that tough but undeniable reality.

2. The utterance of the terms "forgotten, forsaken" in Lamentations 5:20 (on which see the same verbs and same sentiment in Isa. 49:14) suggests that the exiles are like "a motherless child," that is, an abandoned, vulnerable orphan. Exile is an act of being orphaned, and many folk now sense themselves in that status. There is no sure home, no old family place, no recognizable family food. I suggest the theme of *rootlessness*, as though we do not belong anywhere. The enormous popularity of Alex Haley's *Roots* came about, I suggest, not because of fascination with our guilt about slavery, but because of resonance with the need to recover connection and genealogy. (On a less dramatic plane, it is astonishing how many people look to Salt Lake City in order to have the Mormons find their ancestors.)

Exiles need to take with them old habits, old customs, old memories, old photographs. The scriptural resources for such uprooted folk, I suggest, are the genealogies that have seemed to us boring and therefore have been skipped over.[18] We have skipped over them, I imagine, either because we thought those old names were not intrinsically interesting, or because we thought they referenced some family other than our own. The recovery of these genealogies could indeed give an index of the mothers and fathers who have risked before us, who have hoped before us, and who continue even now to believe in us and hope for us. The genealogies might be useful in the recovery of baptism, because in that act, we join a new family. We are like any new in-law at a first family reunion when we meet all the weird uncles and solicitous aunts, who seem like an undifferentiated mass until they are linked with lots of stories.[19] After the stories are known, the list becomes meaningful and is simply shorthand that makes and keeps the stories available. Two easy access points for such genealogy are (a) the Matthean genealogy, which includes some of our most scandalous mothers (Matt. 1:1–17), and (b) the recital in Hebrews 11 of all our family "by faith."

The texts serve to overcome the isolation of the orphan and our sense of "motherless" existence, by giving us the names of mothers and fathers and by situating us in a "communion of saints" who are the living dead who continue to watch over us. I suggest that if the genealogical indices are well handled, they become a way to recover old narratives that contextualize our present faith. When well done, moreover, local congregations can extend the list, not only of members of their own congregation, but of folk known publicly, beyond the congregation, who have risked for and shaped faith. It is inevitable that with this evocation of gratitude to those on the list, we enter our names on the same list with a sense of accountability, and begin to understand what it might mean to have our own names written in "the book of life."[20]

3. The most obvious reality and greatest threat to exiles is the *power of despair*. On the one hand, everything for which we have worked is irretrievably lost. On the other hand, we are helpless in this circumstance and fated here forever. In ancient Israel, this despair of a theological kind is rooted in two "failures of faith." First, Israel doubts *God's fidelity*, that is, God's capacity to care and remember (cf. Lam. 5:20, quoted in Isa. 49:14). Second, Israel doubts *God's power* to save, even if God remembers (cf. Isa. 50:2; 59:1). On both counts, Israel has concluded that in its exile, it is without a God who makes any difference and is therefore hopelessly in the grip of the perpetrators of exile.

The scriptural resource against this despair is voiced especially in Isaiah 40—55. This is a text well known to us, if for no other reason than that Handel has made it available to us. Very often, however, critical study of this text has been focused on distracting questions, like "Who is the Suffering Servant?" Leaders of exilic communities in despair, as I suspect some of us are, would do better to focus on the primary intent of the poetry, namely, that God's powerful resolve is to transform the debilitating reality of exile. Of the rich resources in this poetry, we may identify especially four motifs voiced as hope against despair:

a. It is this poetry that transforms the word "gospel" into a theological term. In 40:9 and 52:7, the "good news" is that Yahweh has triumphed over the power of exile, that is, over Babylonian gods (cf. 46:1–4) and over Babylonian royal power (47:1–11). As a result, Israel's self-definition need not be derived from that harsh, seemingly permanent regime.

b. It is II Isaiah's words that explode the faith of Israel into creation faith (cf. 40:12–17; 42:5; 44:24). Now the scope of God's saving power is not a "nickel and dime" operation in Israel, but the whole of global reality is viewed as a resource whereby God's transformative action is mobilized on behalf of this little, needy community. In this poetry, creation is not an end in itself, but an instrument of rescue. Israel is urged to "think big" and to "sing big" about the forces of life at work on its behalf.

c. Speeches of judgment show God, as construed by this poet, engaged in a heavy-handed dispute with Babylonian gods, in order to delegitimate their claims, and to establish the proper claims of Yahwistic faith (41:21–29; 44:6–7; 45:20–21). The purpose of such rhetorical action is to give Israel "spine," to enable Israel not to give up its covenantal identity for the sake of its ostensive masters. That is, Israel is invited to chutzpah in holding to its own peculiar identity.

d. This defiant speech against the other, phony gods is matched by an affirmative tenderness expressed in salvation oracles (41:13, 14–16; 43:1–5). Rolf Rendtorff and Rainer Albertz have noticed that "creation language" is used in salvation oracles, not to refer to "the creation of the world," but for the creation of Israel who is God's treasured creature.[21] As is often recognized, Isaiah 43:1–5 articulates something like baptismal phrasing: "I have called you by name, you are mine." That baptismal language, however, is cast in creation speech forms.

This combination of defiance and tenderness indicates that Israel's seemingly helpless present is teeming with liberating and intentionality. Israel is expected, in this poetry, to cease its mesmerized commitment to the rulers of this age (here Babylon), who thrive on the despair of Israel, and to receive through this poetry the freedom of imagination to act "as" a people headed "home."[22] In our contemporary circumstance of ministry, I suggest that despair is the defining pathology that robs the church of missional energy and of stewardship generosity. The poet who uttered these words has dared to voice an originary option against all the visible evidence. But then, faith is precisely and characteristically "the assurance of things hoped for, the conviction of things not seen" (Heb. 11:1). As long as the exiles hope for nothing and are convinced of nothing unseen, it is guaranteed that they will stay in thrall to Babylon. The poet refuses such a pitiful, shameful abandonment of identity.

4. Exile is an experience of *profaned absence*. The "absence of God" is not only a personal, emotional sense, but a public, institutional awareness that "the glory has departed." In ancient Israel this sense had to do with the destruction of the temple, the departure of God from Jerusalem (cf. Ezekiel 9—10) so that God "had no place," and the abusive handling of temple vessels, so that the very "vehicles for God" were treated like a tradable commodity.[23]

In our time, it is clear that what have long been treasured symbols are treated lightly or with contempt. (I suspect that this is what is entailed in the great passion generated by "flag burning" and "bra burning," and such acts of defiance against "sacred order.") Many people have concluded with chagrin that "nothing is sacred anymore." With the absence of God, larger "meanings" become impossible. And because God is absent, we become increasingly selfish and brutalizing, because without God, "everything is possible." (No doubt popular, "right-wing" religion trades effectively on this sense of loss.)

Unfortunately, critical scholarship (and especially Protestant usage) have neglected the texts that pertain to the "crisis of presence" which are found especially in the "Priestly texts" of the Pentateuch.[24] With our deep-set Protestant resistance to any sacramentalism that sounds automatic and/or routine, the Priestly texts have been treated by us with a rather consistent lack of interest, if not disdain.

It is important to us, in our exilic situation, to renotice that these texts constitute a major pastoral response to the exilic crisis of absence. I suggest that these texts might be useful resources for ministry, if we understand them as a recovery of sacrament as a way to "host the holy" in a context of profane absence. The priests had no inclination, or found it impossible, to affirm that God was everywhere loose in the exile of Babylon. Indeed, a case could be made in priestly perception that God would refuse to be available in such a miserable context as Babylon. Where then might God be? The answer is, in the sacramental life of Israel, so that God becomes a counterpresence to Babylonian profanation. The reason for coming to "the holy place" is to come into "the presence," which is everywhere else precluded in this exile that is under hostile management.

I suggest three aspects of this recovery of the sacramental, plus a footnote: (a) Central to the sacramental life of Israel was *circumcision* (cf. Genesis 17). To be sure, that powerful cultic act is profoundly patriarchal. In the exile, however, it becomes a rich and larger metaphor for faith (cf. Deut. 10:16; 30:6; Jer. 4:4). Moreover, the "marking" of circumcision is transposed in Christian practice into baptism, which, like circumcision, is a mark of distinctiveness. It distinguishes its subjects from the definitions of the empire, even if the Babylonians cannot see it. (b) *Sabbath* emerges as a primal act of faith in exile. I understand the Sabbath to be a quiet but uncompromising refusal to be defined by the production system of Babylon, so that life is regularly and with discipline enacted as a trusted gift and not as a frantic achievement. (c) Most important, the *tabernacle* is an imaginative effort to form a special place where God's holiness can be properly hosted and therefore counted upon (Exodus 25—31, 35—40; cf. Ezekiel 40—48 on an exilic concern for cultic presence). I am not convinced that this text of Exodus 25—31, 35—40 describes any concrete, practiced reality in exilic Israel. It may be nothing more than a textual fantasy. Nonetheless, it is a fantasy about presence, about the willingness of the exodus God to sojourn midst this displaced people of the wilderness. While God is thus willing to occupy and visit a disestablished people, the presence of God is not casual or haphazard. It requires discipline and care that is almost punctilious.

It is thoroughly biblical to attend to modes of presence that are visible (material, physical) so that the whole of presence is not verbal (or sermonic). I understand the reasons that conventional Protestantism has avoided such modes of thought and practice. Such a resistance was necessary in order to break the terrible and destructive power of the old sacramentalism in the sixteenth century. It is the case, however, that our present "exilic" crisis is not marked by a threat of "popish sacramentalism," as in the sixteenth century. Our threat rather is a technological emptiness that is filled by the liturgies of consumerism and commoditization. The issue in our own context is whether holy presence can be received, imagined, and practiced in ways that counteract that powerful, debilitating ideology. It is clear that the letter to the Hebrews (chapters 7—10) does not flinch from thinking christologically in terms of tabernacle presence. I suspect that for exiles, a verbal presence by itself is too thin, which is why the Priestly materials came to dominate the canon. It is also why Reformed faith in the magisterial tradition may want to make ecumenical moves to reengage the very sacramentalism it scuttled. Exiles who live in a profaned context have a deep need to "touch and handle" things unseen.

5. Exile is an experience of *moral incongruity*. That is, the displacement and destructiveness of exile make one aware that the terrible fate of displacement is more massive than can be explained in terms of moral symmetry. The classic biblical response to exile is that exile is punishment from God for the violation of torah. Such a guilt-focused interpretation does indeed keep the world morally coherent and reliable. But at enormous cost! The cost of protecting God's moral reliability is to take the blame for very large disorders. This sense of "blame," in my judgment, exacts too high a cost for moral symmetry, and so produces the practical problem of theodicy, the awareness that this "evil" cannot be explained by or contained in our "fault." Something else besides our "fault" is loose and at work in the destabilizing of our world.[25]

In the Old Testament, the problem of theodicy, that is, the thought that God is implicated in a morally incoherent world, surfaces in the book of Job. While the book of Job cannot be securely tied to the context of exile, most scholars believe it belongs there, and many believe it is a direct and intentional response to the oversimplification of retribution theology.[26]

Mutatis mutandis, the problem of theodicy belongs appropriately to our own exilic circumstance. If exile is understood as "the failure of the established church," it is difficult to think that this failure is "our fault," for the forces of secularism are larger than we are, and it does little good to blame somebody. If exile is understood as "the failure of the white, male, Western hegemony," it is difficult to take the blame as a white male, even if one is generically implicated. The book of Job is able to entertain in any exile, including ours, that something more is at work than fault, so that our circumstance of exile is not easily reduced to moral symmetry.

I think that the honest surfacing of this issue of theodicy, in Joban terms, would be a liberating act among us. It is an act that fully acknowledges moral asymmetry, that does not reduce reality to "score keeping," that refuses to accept all the blame, and that dares to entertain the unsettled thought of God's failure. In the poem of Job, both the terrible indictment of God (9:13–24) and the confident self-affirmation of Job (29—31) prepare the way for the whirlwind that blows away all moral issues (38:1–42:6). In the extremity of exile, I believe it would be an important pastoral gain to have the whirlwind obliterate and blow away many of our all-consuming moral questions. In the poem of Job, the questions of failure, fault, blame, and guilt simply evaporate. We are invited to a larger vista of mystery that contains wild and threatening dimensions of faith. The poem extricates Israel from the barrenness of moral explanation and justification and thinks instead of dangerous trust and affirmation in a context where we cannot see our way through. The world of Job is filled with wondrous crocodiles (41:1–34) and hippopotamuses (40:15–24) along with cunning evil; deep, unanswered questions; and vigorous doxology.

It is also a world where, through the dismay, gifts are given and life inexplicably goes on (42:7–17). If Job is misunderstood as an intellectual enterprise, it may cut the nerve of faith. But if it is taken as a pastoral opportunity to explode petty, narcissistic categories for a larger field of mystery, it might indeed enable exiles to embrace their self-concern and then move past it to larger, more dangerous dimensions of living in an unresolvable and inexplicable world where God's mystery overrides all our moral programs.

6. The danger in exile is to become so preoccupied with self that one cannot get outside one's self to rethink, reimagine, and redescribe larger reality. Self-preoccupation seldom yields energy, courage, or freedom. In ancient Israel, one of the strategies for coping shrewdly and responsibly beyond self were the narratives of defiance and cunning that enjoined exiles not to confront their harsh overlords directly, but to negotiate knowingly between faith and the pressures of "reality."[27]

If we can get past difficult critical problems, we may take some such narratives as models and invitations for living freely, dangerously, and tenaciously in a world where faith does not have its own way. Smith shows how these narratives perform a crucial strategic function and includes in his analysis the tales of Joseph, Esther, and Daniel. We may comment briefly upon these resources:

a. The story of Joseph concerns the capacity of an Israelite to cooperate fully with the established regime (perhaps too fully), but to maintain at the same time an edge of discernment that permits him to look out for his folk. He does not fully adopt the "reality" defined by his overlords.

b. The tale of Esther shows a courageous Jew willing and able to outflank established power, to gain not only honor for herself but well-being for her people.

c. The story of Daniel shows a young man pressed into the civil service of the empire, able to exercise authority in the empire precisely because he maintained a sense of self rooted quite outside the empire.

This practice of narrative admits of no easy "Christ against culture" model, but recognizes the requirement of an endlessly cunning, risky process of negotiation. Such negotiations may seem to purists to be too accommodationist. And to accommodationists, they may seem excessively scrupulous. If, however, assimilation into the dominant culture is a major threat for exiles, the lead characters of these narratives do not forget who they are, with whom they belong, nor the God whom they serve. I imagine many baptized exiles must live such a life of endless negotiation. These narratives might name and clarify the process and tilt self-perception toward membership in the faithful community. The stunning characters in these narratives are indeed "bilingual," knowing the speech of the empire and being willing to use it, but never forgetting the cadences of their "mother tongue."

Preaching to Exiles

It is clear that "exile" is a rich and supple metaphor. As the biblical writers turned the metaphor of exile in various and imaginative directions, so may we. Note well, I have made no argument about the one-to-one match between metaphor and reality. I have proposed only that this metaphor mediates our experience to us in fresh ways and gives access to scriptural resources in equally fresh ways.

There are two by-products in the utilization of a countermetaphor that I will mention. On the one hand, pondering this metaphor helps us think again about a rich variety of metaphors in scripture that can function as a kaleidoscope, to let us see our life and faith in various dimensions, aspects, angles, and contexts. Such an exercise may move us past a single, frozen metaphor that we take as a permanent given. On the other hand, the availability of a countermetaphor that opens us to a plurality of metaphors helps us notice that our usual, "taken-for-granted" world is also a metaphorical construct, even if an unrecognized or unacknowledged one. That is, post-modern awareness helps us to consider that there is no "given reality" behind our several constructs, but even our presumed given reality is itself a rhetorical construct, whether of the cold war, or consumer capitalism, or the "free world," or the male hegemony, or whatever.[28] An awareness of this reality about "world" and about "self" opens the way to liminality that permits transformation of all those "givens."[29]

1. In the argument I have made, there are important interpretive issues to be considered by the preacher. I suggest that the Bible be understood as a set of models (paradigms) of reality made up of images situated in and contextualized by narratives.[30] These narrative renderings of reality in the Bible (as elsewhere) are not factual reportage, but are inevitably artistic constructs that stand a distance from any "fact" and are filtered through interest of a political kind. I think it a major gain to see that the Bible in its several models is an artistic, rhetorical proposal of reality that seeks to persuade (convert) to an alternative sense of God, world, neighbor, and self.

2. As there are interpretive implications to the argument I have made, so there are also crucial ecclesial implications in construing life through the metaphor of exile. This literary, rhetorical focus invites the baptismal community to construe its place in the world differently, and I imagine, faithfully.[31] The engagement with this metaphor may deliver pastors and people from magisterial notions of being (or needing to be) chaplains for the establishment and guardians of stable public forms of life.

I understand the liberty given through this metaphor quite practically and concretely. As the preacher stands up to preach among the exiles, the primal task (given this metaphor) concerns the narration and nurture of a counteridentity, the enactment of the power of hope in a season of despair, and the assertion of a deep, definitional freedom from the pathologies, coercions, and seductions that govern our society. The preacher is not called upon to do all the parts of public policy and public morality, but to give spine, resolve, courage, energy, and freedom that belong to a counter-identity.

As the congregation listens and participates in this odd construal of reality, the metaphor might also make a decisive difference in the listening. The working woman or man knows that "it is a jungle out there" and that one without a resilient, resistant identity can indeed be eaten alive. The teenager off to school is in the rat race of success and popularity, let alone competence and adequacy. And now every man, woman, and child is invited to a zone of freedom that the dominant culture cannot erode. That zone of freedom is grounded in what the baptized know:

> That our sense of *loss and sadness* is serious and honorable, and
> one need not prop up or engage in denial.

That our *rootedness* enables us to belong, so that we are not
swept away by every wind of doctrine, every market seduction, or every economic coercion, knowing who we are.

That the promises of the creator surge in our life and in our
world, so that the *manipulatable despair* of the hopeless,
which turns folk into commodity consumers, is not the live
edge of our existence.

That there is a *holy, awesome presence* that persists against the
emptied profanation of promiscuous economic and lustful
sexuality, that true *desire* is for the presence that overrides all
of our trivialized desires that are now robbed of authority.

That the world is *not morally coherent*, but there is a deep
incongruity in which we live, that we need neither to resolve,
explain, or deny. A raw, ragged openness is linked to the
awesome reality of God's holiness.

That we are always about to be domesticated; we have these
narrative models of resistance, defiance, and negotiation that remind us that there is more to life than conformist obedience
or shameful accommodation. We know the names of those
who have faced with freedom the trouble that is caused by
faith.

3. There is nothing in this faith model of "sectarian withdrawal" of
the kind of which Stanley Hauerwas and William H. Willimon are often
accused.[32] The baptized do indeed each day find themselves finally in
the presence of those who preside over the exile, that is, in the presence
of "Babylonians." They are unavoidable, even in this model, or especially in this model. This baptismal identity is not designed for a ghetto
existence. It is rather intended for full participation in the life of the
dominant culture, albeit with a sense of subversiveness that gives
unnerving freedom.

Jeremiah knew about the dangers of withdrawal from dominant culture.
For that reason, in his letter to the exiles, the prophet encourages the exiles
with amazing, endlessly problematic words:[33]

> But seek the welfare (*shalom*) of the city where I have sent you into
> exile, and pray to the LORD on its behalf, for in its welfare (*shalom*)
> you will find your welfare (*shalom*). (Jer. 29:7)

There is no "separate peace" for exiles, no private deals with God, no
permitted withdrawal from the affairs of the empire. The only *shalom*
these troubled Jews would know is the *shalom* wrought for Babylon. The
letter implies that the exiled community of Jews can indeed impact Babylon
with *shalom* through its active concern and prayer, but only as the

community knows that it is not Babylon. The distance from Babylon makes possible an impacting nearness to Babylon.

4. Finally, but not too soon, the preacher's theme for exiles is homecoming. The home promised to the exiles, however, is not any nostalgic return to yesteryear, for that home is irreversibly gone. Rather, the home for which the exiles yearn and toward which they hope is the "kingdom of God," an arena in which God's good intention is decisive. The New Testament struggles to speak concretely about that realm and can do so only indirectly and by allusion, for that realm lies beyond all our known categories.

It is no stretch to link *homecoming* to *gospel* to *kingdom*. The linkage is already made in Isaiah 40—55 and in Ezekiel 37:1–14. It is telling that Karl Barth speaks of the "obedience of the Son of God" under the rubric of "The Way of the Son of God into a Far Country."[34] The textual allusion is of course to the Prodigal Son, though Barth's accent is on the "emptying and humiliation" of Jesus, as in Philippians 2:5–11.[35] Conversely, in speaking of the exaltation of Jesus, Barth writes of "the Homecoming of the Son of Man."[36] An important critique may be made of Barth's usage, for it reflects his characteristic transcendentalism, whereby the course of human existence is by definition exile. It is my intention to suggest that the metaphor of exile/homecoming that Barth handles christologically, and that Buber handles philosophically, be understood among us ecclesiologically with reference to the concrete realities of economics, politics, and social relations.

Consider, then, what it means to be exiles awaiting and hoping for homecoming to the kingdom of God! In the Bible, the image of "Kingdom of God" is stitched together by narratives of miracle and wonder, whereby God does concrete acts of transformation that the world judges to be impossible. The "Kingdom" is a time and place and context in which God's "impossibilities" for life, joy, and wholeness are all made possible and available.[37] In the meantime, the waiting, hoping exiles are fixed upon these impossibilities. In so doing, the exiles refuse the world's verdict on the impossibilities, and, as a result, they pay less heed and allegiance to the world's wearisome possibilities. The alternative to this subversive entry into the world is to accept the world's possibilities as the only chance for the future. Such a decision rejects the miracles of God and so enters endlessly into the seductive land of exile. Failing the countervision of the gospel, we will no doubt "labor for that which does not satisfy" (Isa. 55:2).

2

Cadences That Redescribe: Speech among Exiles

Exile, that is social, cultural displacement, is not primarily geographical but liturgical and symbolic.[1] This was the case with the Jews in exile in the sixth century B.C.E., as it is in our Western culture presently. In defining exile, Alan Mintz writes that

> the catastrophic element in events [of exile] is defined as the power to shatter the existing paradigms of meaning, especially as regards the bonds between God and the people of Israel.[2]

In such a situation where "paradigms of meaning" are shattered, it is clear that exiles must pay careful and sustained attention to speech, because it requires inordinately disciplined and imaginative speech to move through the shattering to newly voiced meaning. Mintz suggests that in exile, the primal speakers (poets) attempt

> first to *represent the catastrophe* and then to *reconstruct, replace, or redraw the threatened paradigm of meaning,* and thereby make creative survival possible.[3]

I find Paul Ricoeur's phrasing a useful way to understand what is required and what is possible for speech in such situations. Ricoeur speaks in terms of "limit experiences" that permit and require "limit expressions."[4] Limit experiences are those in which all conventional descriptions and explanations are inadequate. When one is pushed experientially to such extremity, one cannot continue to mouth commonplaces but is required to utter something "odd."[5] The odd limit expression is in language that effectively *redescribes* reality away from and apart from all usual assumptions about reality.[6] Thus such speech invites the speaker and the listener into a world that neither had known before this utterance.

It is clear that in exile, while something utterly new must be uttered, that is, not contained within or regulated by past utterance, this daring speech which evokes newness nonetheless employs in fresh ways speech that is already known and trusted. In order to serve as "redescription," however, the already trusted speech must be uttered in daring, venturesome ways that intensify, subvert, and amaze.

By utilizing the theme of exile as an analogue by which to describe (redescribe?) our current social situation in the West, I suggest that our loss of the white, male, Western, colonial hegemony, which is deeply displacing for us, is indeed a limit experience whereby we are pushed to the edge of our explanatory and coping powers. Such experience requires limit expression. Such a consideration is appropriate for preachers precisely because preachers in such a limit experience have obligation and possibility of being the very ones who can give utterance both to "represent the catastrophe" and to "reconstruct, replace, or redraw" the paradigms of meaning that will permit "creative survival." I suggest that the preaching task now is nothing less than that twofold task.

In what follows I will consider four examples of limit expression that were utilized in that ancient exile of sixth-century Jews, in order that their limit experience of displacement could be embraced and moved through. My thought is that there are clues here for our own speech practice in a time of acute displacement and bewilderment.

Lamentation and Complaint

The first task among exiles is to represent the catastrophe, to state what is happening by way of loss in vivid images so that the loss can be named by its right name and so that it can be publicly faced in the depth of its negativity. Such naming and facing permits the loss to be addressed to God, who is implicated in the loss as less than faithful in a context seen to be one of fickleness and failure. Such speech requires enough candor to dare to utter the torrent of sensitivities that cluster, such as pain, loss, grief, shame, and rage. For this naming and facing, of course, this ancient Jewish community found its best speech by appeal to the liturgic tradition of *lamentation* (which expresses sadness) and *complaint* (which expresses indignation).[7]

The richest, most extreme statement of sadness, punctuated by loss, helplessness, and vulnerability, is the book of Lamentations.[8] It is not much studied or used among us, no doubt because it has seemed so remote from our cultural situation. If, however, we are now in a new situation of profound loss, as I have suggested, this poetry could be for us an important "speech resource." The little book of Lamentations consists of five extended poems of grief over the destruction of Jerusalem (for which I have suggested as an analogue the loss of our accustomed privilege and certitude). In the first poem (chapter 1), the bereft city of Jerusalem is "like a widow," abandoned, shamed, vulnerable, subject to abuse, without an advocate or defender (1:1). The recurring theme of the abandonment of Jerusalem is expressed as "no one to comfort her" (vv. 2, 9, 16, 17), "no resting place" (v. 3), "no pasture" (v. 6), "no one to help" (v. 7). The imagery is of a woman overwhelmed with tears, under assault, and subject to abuse.[9] While there is in 3:21–33 a powerful statement of hope and confidence, the collection of Lamentations ends with a sense of "forsakenness":

> Why have you *forgotten* us completely?
> Why have you *forsaken* us these many days?
> (Lam. 5:20)

This same sense of being "forgotten" is evident in the more abrasive and indignant complaint of Psalm 74. The poet is more aggressive here in describing to God the situation of dismay and in pressing God to act.[10] The poem provides for God a play-by-play of what "your foes" have done to "your holy place" (v. 4; cf. vv. 4–9). It then moves to a doxology (see below), recalling to God God's own powerful miracles of the past (vv. 12–17). These concern God's sovereign rule over all of creation, and God's capacity to bring life out of chaos. By juxtaposing the present calamity of the temple and God's glorious past, the poem makes intercession that God should now act, both to defeat the impious enemies and to ensure that "the downtrodden are not put to shame" (v. 21; cf. vv. 18–23). One is struck in this psalm with the directness of speech, the candor about the current trouble, which is catastrophic, and the vigor with which God is expected to act in fidelity.

Through both the lamentation and the psalm of complaint, the catastrophic is vividly represented to make it as palpable to God as it is to the community. My suggestion, insofar as our current Western dismay is a parallel to this ancient travesty, is that a primary pastoral task is to voice the felt loss, indignation, and bewilderment that are among us. The reason extreme imagery is required is that the speech must cut through the enormous self-deception of political/economic euphemism. For the truth is that the old, settled advantage in the world upon which we have counted is over and gone, as over and gone as was Jerusalem's temple. Sadness, pain, and indignation are not inappropriate responses to the loss, either then or now. They require abrasive, insistent speech to be available, and ancient Israel gives us a script for our own daring representation of the trouble.

Assurance

In the laments and complaints, Israel speaks to God. Israel takes the initiative in rightly naming its displacement to God. In times of debili-

tating dismay, it is the one who experiences the dismay who must coura-
geously come to speech.[11] This is abundantly clear in the speech of ancient Israel. But Israel's limit expressions are not restricted to the voice
of Israel. The voice of Yahweh also sounds in the daring rhetoric of the
exile, precisely in the context where Israel had sensed its abandonment
by God. Indeed, in the poetry of II Isaiah, God acknowledges that God
has been silent too long and will now break that silence in powerful
speech. God says,

> For a long time I have held my peace,
>   I have kept still and restrained myself;
> now I will cry out like a woman in labor,
>   I will gasp and pant.[12]
>   (Isa. 42:14; cf. 62:1)

In the "salvation oracles" of II Isaiah, Israel hears the classic assurance
that God is present with and for Israel, even in its dismay and displacement.
Most precisely and succinctly, this oracle of assurance asserts on God's lips,
"Fear not, for I am with you" (cf. Isa. 41:13, 14; 43:1–5; 44:8; Jer.
30:10–11).[13] Joseph Sittler among others has seen that this speech is closely
paralleled to the way a parent reassures a child who has had a nightmare.[14]
Such parental assurance is indeed a redescription. Indeed, this assurance is
a nightmare-ending speech, for it asserts a caring presence that is trusted
enough and powerful enough to override the sense of absence evoked by
the exile. Now, in this utterance, what had seemed to be a place of absence
is known to be a place of presence, thereby invested with great potential
for life.

While the salvation oracle proper is highly stylized, Claus Westermann
has seen that there are great variations on the theme of assurance expressed
in a variety of forms, including what he calls "assurance of salvation,"
"announcement of salvation," and "portrayal of salvation."[15] We do not
need to pay too close attention to the variations in form. What counts for
our consideration is the situation-transforming capacity of the utterance,
what Ricoeur would term "redescription."

Thus Lamentations 5:20 ends with haunting sense of being "forgotten"
and "forsaken":

> Why have you *forgotten* us completely?
>   Why have you *forsaken* us these many days?

In Isaiah 49:14, the same two terms are reiterated (probably deliberately
quoted):

> But Zion said, "The Lord has *forsaken* me,
>   my Lord has *forgotten* me."

But then in Isaiah 49:15–16, these haunting fearful questions are answered by the God who does not forget or abandon:

> Can a woman *forget* her nursing child,
>   or show no compassion for the child of her womb?
> Even these may *forget*,
>   yet I will not *forget* you.
> See, I have inscribed you on the palms of my hands;
>   your walls are continually before me.

Or in Isaiah 54:10, after conceding that there had been a brief aban-donment of Israel by God (vv. 7–8), and after comparing the devastation of the exile to the flood in Genesis (v. 9), the poet has God utter a sweeping assurance of God's reliable durability:[16]

> For the mountains may depart and the hills be removed,
> but my *steadfast love* shall not depart from you,
>   and my *covenant of peace* shall not be removed,
>   says the LORD, who has *compassion* on you.
>
>   (Isa. 54:10)

This triad of Yahweh's characteristics—steadfast love, covenant of peace, and compassion—is more than enough to override the flood, to overcome the absence and shame, and to overmatch the terror of exile.

We are so familiar with sure assurances that we may fail to notice what a daring act of faith such an utterance is, how blatantly it speaks against and be-yond perceived circumstance in order to "reconstruct, replace, or redraw the threatened paradigm of meaning." It is an act of powerful faith on the part of the speaker but also on the part of the listener. The intent of the assurance is to create faith in the listener. The exile was widely seen to be a season of God's absence, and now this poet dares to assert that God is present in that very cir-cumstance, faithfully at work to bring a newness out of the defeat.

The analogue in our own time is for the preacher-poet of the gospel to make such an utterance in the midst of our failed privilege and hegemony. The utterance of assurance is not to prop up the old paradigm, for the assurance comes only after the "representation of the catastrophe," that is, after the felt and expressed situation of lamentation and complaint. The assurance asserts that in the very midst of economic displacement and bewilderment about sexuality, where all old certitudes are in profound jeopardy, just these meanings of a new kind are being wrought by the power and fidelity of God, "new things" shaped like covenantal faithful-ness that will become visible only in, with, and through the displacement.[17] Such utterances are indeed "by faith alone." But then, that is always how the gospel is uttered in such problematic circumstance.

Doxologies of Defiance

The counterpoint to lamentation and complaint is the hymn of praise that emerges from "victory songs." Hymns are sung when situations of great trouble are transformed by the power and mercy of God. Israel has been singing such songs since the deliverance from Egypt (Ex. 15:1–18, 21). These daring doxologies sing what Israel has seen and heard about the decisive power and reliable commitment of Yahweh to intrude in life-giving ways in circumstances of defeat, disorder, and death. Thus the doxology of remembrance in Psalm 74:12–17 reaches all the way back to creation and to God's capacity to order chaos. And the despondent worshiper in Psalm 77:11–20 ponders the remembered exodus. Out of these treasured, concrete memories, Israel's hymns also constitute acts of hope and confidence that what God has done in the past is what God will do in the present and in the future.

In the exile, the doxologies are not primarily acts of remembering God's past "wonders" but anticipatory assertions concerning what God is about to do. Israel is summoned to sing a "new song," to sing praise for God's sovereign liberating action that is now about to occur (Isa. 42:10).

In the situation of exile in Babylon, it was "self-evident" that the Babylonian gods had triumphed, that Yahweh had failed, either because of weakness or because of indifference. Either way, the evidence suggested that loyalty to Yahweh no longer worked or was worth practicing, because other powers could give more reliable and immediate payoffs.

The poetry of II Isaiah, however, will not accept the "self-evident" reading of reality. The hymns offered by the poet are assertions against the evident, insisting that Yahweh's saving power is at the break of new activity. Thus, Israel has concluded that God does not care about Israel:

> Why do you say, O Jacob,
>   and speak, O Israel,
> "My way is hidden from the LORD,
>   and my right is disregarded by my God"?
>   (Isa. 40:27)

The responding hymn of verses 28–31 asserts in wondrous lyric that Yahweh is the God of all generations, past, present, future, and is not weary or faint or powerless but gives power to those who hope. The outcome is not only a statement about God but an assurance to those who trust this God:

> [T]hose who wait for the LORD shall renew their strength,
>   they shall mount up with wings like eagles,
> they shall run and not be weary,
>   they shall walk and not faint.
>   (Isa. 40:31)

Notice that the doxology completely rejects the notion of the rule of the Babylonian gods. Against their apparent rule, it is, so the hymn asserts, in fact Yahweh who holds power and who gives power (cf. 46:1–4).

That same contrast is evident in the defiant doxology of Isaiah 41:21–29. Negatively the gods of Babylon are called to give account of themselves, and they fail miserably (vv. 21–23). This leads to the conclusion that they are nothing, nothing at all. Moreover, those who trust such "nothing gods" are as "nothing" as their gods.

> You, indeed, are nothing
> and your work is nothing at all;
> whoever chooses you is an abomination.
> (Isa. 41:24)

Positively, it is Yahweh who is able to act visibly, decisively, and trans-formatively (vv. 25–27). Israel's doxologies are characteristically against the data, inviting Israel to live in a "redescribed world," in which meaning has been "reconstructed, replaced, or redrawn."

In our own situation, the hymnic act of praise has become largely innocuous. It happens often among us that the praise is either escapist fantasy, or it is a bland affirmation of the status quo. In fact, doxology is a daring political, polemical act that serves to dismiss certain loyalties and to embrace and legitimate other loyalties and other shapes of reality.[18]

In the context of II Isaiah, the hymnic wager is on Yahweh's intention for homecoming, and therefore on the refusal of the Babylonian gods who seek to define the world in noncovenantal ways. In our situation of up-heaval and confusion, hymns that celebrate the God of the Bible wager on a covenantal-neighborly world powered by the neighborliness of God, and wager against any characterization of the world that bets on selfishness, greed, fear, abuse, or despair. Our current world of bewilderment is often described as though everything good is ending, as though the forces of chaos have won. This hymnic tradition authorizes the church to identify and redescribe this present place as the arena in which the rule of the creator-liberator God is working a wondrous newness. Our singing and utterance of such lyrical faith assert that we will not submit to the gods of fear and anticovenantal power relations. In such a situation as ours, the words and music for a "new song" are acts of powerful renewal.

Promises

The assurances and hymns upon which we have commented are antici-patory. They look to the resolve of Yahweh to work a newness that is not yet visible or in hand. Exiles, however, have a way of speech that is more directly and singularly preoccupied with God's sure future, namely, oracles of promise. Israel believes that God can indeed work a newness out of present shambles and that that newness will more fully embody God's goodwill for the world. It is cause for amazement that Israel's most daring and definitional promises were uttered in exile, that is, precisely when the evidence seems to preclude such hope. The promises are assertions that God is not a prisoner of circumstance but that God can call into existence that which does not exist (cf. Rom. 4:17).

Here I will cite three of the best-known and most powerful of such exilic promises. In Jeremiah 31:31–34 the promise asserts that God will work a new covenant with Israel that is aimed at torah obedience (v. 33) but is rooted in the overriding reality of forgiveness (v. 34).[19] The dominant assumption about exile in the Old Testament, propounded especially in the Deuteronomic tradition, is that exile is punishment (2 Kings 17:7–23; see even Isa. 40:2). This promise, in the face of a theology of guilt-and-punishment, is an assertion that forgiveness will overpower sin, and Israel's primal theological reality is the future-creating graciousness of Yahweh who will "remember their sin no more."[20]

In Ezekiel 37:1–14, the prophet Ezekiel searches for an adequate metaphor for exile and homecoming. The most extreme imagery available is that exile equals death. From death, there is no hope, for the power of death is strong and decisive. In a radical, rhetorical break, however, the prophet dares to assert that by the power of God's spirit, "I will open your graves"; that is, "I will place you on your own soil" (vv. 13–14). Exile is not the last word; that is, death is not the last reality. Israel's situation is not hopeless, because God's transformative wind (spirit) blows even in the dismay of exile, in order to work a newness toward life.

The poem of Isaiah 65:17–25 (which may be dated slightly after the return from exile in 520 B.C.E.) offers a "portrayal of salvation" in stunning anticipatory fashion. The poet anticipates a new earth and a new Jerusalem characterized by new social relations, new economic possibilities, and new communion with God. Indeed, the poet foresees a complete and concrete inversion of Israel's current situation of hopelessness.

Notice that all of the promises, specific as they are, are cast as God's own speech, the authority for which is not found in any visible circumstance but in the trustworthiness of the God who speaks. It is God's own resolve to work a newness that will impinge upon what seems to be a closed, hopeless situation.

Exiles inevitably must reflect upon the power of promise, upon the capacity of God to work a newness against all circumstance.[21] Promise has become nearly an alien category among us. That is partly an intellectual problem for us, because our Enlightenment perception of reality does not believe that there can be any newness "from the outside" that can enter our fixed world. The loss of promise is also a function of our privilege in the world, whereby we do not in fact want newness, but only an enhancement and guarantee of our preferred present tense.

As white, male, Western privilege comes to an end, some are likely to experience that "ending" as terrible loss that evokes fear and resentment.[22] Evangelical faith, however, dares to identify what is (for some) an alienating circumstance as the matrix for God's newness (for all). Thus evangelical speech functions to locate the hunches and hints and promises that seem impossible to us that God will indeed work in the midst of our frightening bewilderment. However, the preacher will work primarily not from visible hints and hunches, precisely because hope is "the conviction of things not seen," a conviction rooted in the trusted character of God.

The Ministry of Language

Speech, or as Mintz terms it, "the ministry of language" is one of the few available resources for exile.[23] Exiles are characteristically stripped of all else except speech. What exiles do is to speak their "mother tongue," that is, the speech learned as children from mother, as a way to maintain identity in a situation that is identity denying.

In that ancient world of displacement, the Jews treasured speech that was "redescriptive" precisely because it was not derived from or sanctioned by the managers of the exile. It was, rather, derived from older speech practice of the covenanted community and sanctioned by the evangelical chutzpah of poets who dared to credit such defiant utterances as complaints, lamentations, assurances, hymns, and promises. These are indeed forms of speech from Israel's "mother tongue."

In the "modernist" church of our time (liberal and conservative), there has been a loss of "mother-speech," partly because of subtle epistemological erosion, and partly because we imagine that other forms of speech are more credible and "make more sense." The truth is, however, that speech other than our own gradually results in the muteness of the church, for we have nothing left to say when we have no way left to say it. Exiles need, first of all and most of all, a place in which to practice liberated speech that does not want or receive the legitimacy of context. I take it that the old "paradigms of meaning" are indeed deeply under threat among us. We can scarcely pretend otherwise. We may learn from our ancestors in faith that in such a context, we must indeed "represent the catastrophe" and then "reconstruct, replace, or redraw" the paradigms of meaning. Both tasks are demanding. It belongs nonetheless to the speakers rooted in this tradition of liberated, defiant, anticipatory speech to take up these tasks. It is in, with, and from such speech that there come "all things new."

3

Preaching as Reimagination

I will explore in this chapter sixteen theses concerning my understanding of evangelical preaching in a quite new cultural, epistemological context.

1. *Ours is a changed preaching situation, because the old modes of church absolutes are no longer trusted.*

I do not say that the church's theological absolutes are no longer trusted. But the *old modes* in which those absolutes have been articulated are increasingly suspect and dysfunctional. In my judgment that is because our old modes are increasingly regarded as patriarchal, hierarchical, authoritarian, and monologic. The mistrust that flies under all these adjectives, however, is in fact because of a growing "suspicion" about the linkage between knowledge and power. The mistrust of conventional authority, now broad and deep in our society, is rooted in the failure of positivism, positivism as either scientific, political, or theological. Many are increasingly aware that "absolute knowledge" most characteristically means agreement of all those permitted in the room.[1] Such "absolutism" in "truth," moreover, characteristically has pretensions to "absolute power" as well, surely an adequate reason for suspicion. Those at the margins of dominating knowledge will no longer permit the practitioners of dominating power to be supervisors of absolute knowledge.

2. *Along with the failure of old modes of articulation, we now face the inadequacy of historical-critical understanding of the biblical text as it has been conventionally practiced.*

I do not say the failure or "bankruptcy" of historical criticism but rather its inadequacy, for historical criticism has become, in scripture study, a version of "modes of absolutism" among the elitely educated. It is increasingly clear that historical criticism has become a handmaiden of certain kinds of power.[2] This refers not only to the control of the agenda through academic politics, but it also recognizes that the rise of criticism is deeply related to the banishment of the "supernatural" and to the dismissal of tradition as a form of truthfulness.[3]

One can note that in academic circles where methodological discussions are conducted, there is a growing tension between old-line historical criticism, which serves to distance the text from the interpreter, and "the emerging criticisms" (sociological, literary, and canonical).[4] A probable generalization can be made that critical scholars who most resist change, and who regard the transfer of social power and influence as only modes of "political correctness," cling most passionately to older modes of historical criticism, whereas scholars who advocate and benefit from redistributions of interpretive power engage in sociological and literary criticism. Indeed, old-line historical criticism is our particular form of "positivism" in the biblical, interpretive guild, thus explaining its share of the suspicion I have more generally noted in thesis 1. I am aware that moves from historical criticism are easily judged to be obscurantism, advocacy, or ideology, but those labels only have such lethal connotations in the context of self-satisfied positivism.

3. *A great new reality for preaching is pluralism in the interpreting community of the local congregation.*

All but the most closed and sheltered liturgic congregations are indomitably heterogeneous.[5] That emerging pluralism, moreover, cannot any longer be overcome by absolute assertion. For such absolute assertion, whether by strong pastoral authority or by denominational dictum, can only serve to excommunicate those who see and take and experience reality otherwise. The more frantic our zeal to maintain the oneness and wholeness of "our truth," the more divisive does such practice become.

An honest facing of pluralism can only be pastorally and usefully engaged by an open-ended adjudication that takes the form of trustful, respectful conversation.[6] Such a conversation is joined with no participant seeking to "convert" the other, and no participant knowing the outcome ahead of time, but only with each entering with full respect for the good faith of others and with willingness to entertain the troublesome thought that new "truth" received together may well be out in front of any of us. I am aware that such an approach sounds like relativism, but an answering "objectivism" is destructive not only of the community, but of any chance to receive new truth together. Preaching thus must be conducted in a context where one make proposals and advocacies, but not conclusions.[7]

4. *Pluralism as the perspective and orientation of the community that hears and interprets is matched by an emerging awareness of the polyvalence of the biblical text.*

Texts are open to many meanings, more than one of which may be legitimate and faithful at the same time. This is evident, in its most simple form, in the awareness that many preachers on any given occasion preach many sermons on the same lectionary texts. While not all such sermons may be legitimate and faithful, many of them would qualify as such, without mutual exclusiveness. Notice that such a polyvalence flies in the face of old-line historical criticism that tried to arrive at "the meaning" of the text.[8]

The claim of polyvalence is an invitation for Christians to relearn from Jewish interpretive tradition.[9] Indeed, Jewish interpretation does not seek to give closure to texts, but can permit many readings to stand side by side, reflecting both the rich density of the text and the freedom of interpretation. Such a way of reading, it is clear, reflects the mode of midrashic interpretation, a Jewish affirmation that the voice of the text is variously heard and is not limited by authorial intent.[10]

It is now suggested, moreover, that midrashic interpretation is strongly, even if unwittingly, reflected in Freud's theory of psychoanalysis and in his practice of dream interpretation.[11] Freud understood that dreams are endlessly open to interpretation. In this regard the reading of dreams is not unlike the reading of texts. At the same time, it is important to note that dreams are no more an unreal fantasy than are texts, but contain a profound truth that is available only upon a rich reading. It is unhelpful for the text interpreter, and therefore the preacher, to give heavy closure to texts, because such a habit does a disservice to text and to listener, both of which are practitioners of multiple readings.

5. *Reality is scripted, that is, shaped and authorized by a text.*

Paul Ricoeur has done the most to show us that reality lives by text.[12] By "text," Ricoeur means written discourse that is no longer in the control of the "author" but makes its own testimony and insists upon interpretation. Interpretation, moreover, is "to appropriate *here and now* the intention of the text."[13] But such here and now intention is not derived from the "author" of the text but from the work within the act of interpretation.

That text may be recognized or invisible. It may be a great religious "classic," a powerful philosophical tradition, or a long-standing tribal conviction.[14] It is an account of reality that the community comes to trust and to take for granted as a "given" that tends to be beyond reexamination. This text "describes" reality in a certain way and shape. In a world where there is more than one text, that is, a world of plurality, one text may describe, but if another text intrudes, it is possible for that second text to "redescribe" reality.[15]

It is important, on the basis of this thesis, for the preacher to recognize that there are no "textless" worlds. Such an assertion may be much disputed; at a practical level, however, it is no doubt true. People come to the preaching moment with texts already in hand that describe the world. The preacher who interprets the text, that is, "appropriates here and now the intention of the text," does not act in a vacuum. There are always rival and competing texts, in the face of which the biblical text may be counter-text that does not primarily describe but that subversively "redescribes" reality.

6. *The dominant scripting of reality in our culture is rooted in the Enlightenment enterprise best associated with René Descartes, John Locke, Thomas Hobbes, and*

Jean-Jacques Rousseau, which has issued in a notion of autonomous individualism, ending in what Philip Rieff calls The Triumph of the Therapeutic.[16]

It is difficult to take in the radical shift of assumptions in "world making" that occurred at the beginning of the seventeenth century.[17] The collapse of the hegemony of medieval Christianity, hastened by the Reformation, the Thirty Years' War, and the rise of science, produced, as Susan Bordo has made clear, a profound anxiety about certitude.[18] It was unmistakably clear that certitude would no longer be found in "the truth of Christ," for confessional divisions had broken that truth. Believers henceforth could appeal only to "reason" guided by the spirit, or the spirit measured by reason, clearly a circular mode of truth. Indeed, Descartes introduced his massive program of doubt as an attempt to link the "new truth" to the claims of Christianity. What emerged was the individual knower as the decontextualized adjudicator of truth.[19]

That autonomy in knowledge, moreover, produced autonomy in action and ethics as well, so that the individual becomes the norm for what is acceptable. The end result is a self-preoccupation that ends in self-indulgence and that drives religion to narcissistic catering and consumerism, to limitless seeking after well-being and pleasure on one's own terms, without regard to any "other" in the community.[20]

While this "scripting of reality" has profound critical thought behind it, the practice of this script is embraced and undertaken by those in modern culture who have no awareness of the "text," of its rootage or intention.[21] Thus it is clear that many folk in our culture who come to preaching events are reliant upon this "text of reality" that is permitted to describe the world. The preacher perforce preaches in a world shaped by this text.

7. *This scripting tradition of the Enlightenment exercises an incredible and pervasive hegemony among us.*

The traditions of the Enlightenment form the governing assumptions of every aspect of our commonly engaged public life:

> In economics this text-generated ideology issues in consumerism, which operates on the claim that "more is better," that "most" will make happy, and that each is entitled to and must have all that each can take, even if at the expense of others. Such a "value system" of course on the face of it must discredit the claims of any "other" who is a competitor for the goods that will make me happy. Television advertising is a primary voice in advocating this view of reality, and television is closely allied with spectator sports, which move in the same direction.[22] Witness the "shoe contracts" of college coaches.

In political affairs, this same ideology is rooted in the privilege of European superiority and colonialism, although in recent time that political dimension of the text has found its primary expression in the notion of *Pax Americana*. That ideology assumes that the world works best if the United States adjudicates from a position of dominant power, which in turn guarantees and endlessly enhances the privileged position of the United States in terms of prosperity and standard of living. Thus the public administration of power guarantees that private capacity to consume without limit. The deepness of this claim is evident in the political requirement of a commitment to a "strong America."

In political affairs, this vision of political hegemony perhaps was given authoritative voice by Elihu Root, secretary of state under Theodore Roosevelt and his expansionist notions. Root in turn was the mentor to Henry Stimson, who moved the United States, almost single-handedly through his advocacy and political mechanizations, to take responsibility for the world.[23] And Stimson in turn was the patron and mentor of the "Wise Men" who guided foreign policy, produced the Cold War, and finally overreached in Vietnam.[24]

But of course the end is not yet. The United States is the remaining superpower and can have it all its own way, so it thinks, finding itself most often on the side of the old colonial powers and allied with the forces of reactionism in order to preserve the old hegemony that goes unexamined.

The Enlightenment text, as practiced in the Euro-American world, thus provides an unchallenged rationale for privilege and advantage in the world in every zone of life. It means not only political ascendancy and economic domination, but it also makes its adherents the norm for virtue. In turn this idea shows up even in the church, where it is assumed that the Western church is the privileged norm by which to test all the rest of the church. In the end, even truth is tied in some way to Western virtue.

This defining text of the West is exceedingly hard on and dismissive of those whose lives do not "measure up" to the norms of competence, productivity, and privilege. This text has resulted in a kind of "social Darwinism" in which the fast, smart, well-connected, and ruthless are the "best" people.[25] And the counterpart is impatience with those who are not so "competent" = productive = righteous. Many of the enormous social problems and social inequities in our society are legitimated by this text.

This definitive text exercises great authority over the imagination, even of those who set out to resist its claim and power. As Karl Marx has seen, it exercises a powerful attraction for those who do not share in its promised benefits but are in fact its victims. Marx's dictum is that "the ideas of the dominant class become the dominant ideas."[26] Marx, moreover, understood well that in the end, the dominant class does not need to exercise force, but holds sway by "hegemonic theatre."[27] I suspect that just now the lottery is a tool of such imagination, which proposes that any may succeed in this system. Is this a great system, or what?!

8. *We now know (or think we know) that human transformation (the way people change) does not happen through didacticism or through excessive certitude, but through the playful entertainment of another scripting of reality that may subvert the old given text and its interpretation and lead to the embrace of an alternative text and its redescription of reality.*

Very few people make important changes in their description of the world abruptly. Most of us linger in wistfulness, notice dissonance between our experience and the old text, and wonder if there is a dimension to it all that has been missed.[28] Most of us will not quickly embrace an alternative that is given us in a coercive way. Such coercion more likely makes us defend the old, and in general causes us to become defensive.

Victor Turner noted that there is an "in-between" time and place in social transformation and relocation that he termed "liminality."[29] Liminality is a time when the old configurations of social reality are increasingly seen to be in jeopardy, but new alternatives are not yet in hand.

What we need for such liminality is a safe place in which to host such ambiguity and to notice the tension and unresolve without pressure but with freedom to see and test alternative textings of reality. It is my impression that much preaching that is excessively urgent and earnest does not pay attention to what we know about how we change or how anyone else may receive change when it is given. The text entrusted to the preachers of the church is all about human transformation, but the characteristic modes of presentation, in many quarters, contradict the claim of the text and are the enemies of transformation.

An inviting, effective alternative does not need to be toned down in its claim or made palatable. It does, however, need to be presented in a way that stops well short of coercion that is threatening and that evokes resistance to hearing or appropriating the new text. Preaching, I suggest, is not only the announcement of the alternative, but it is also the practice of that very liminality that does not yet know too much.

9. *The biblical text, in all its odd disjunctions, is an offer of an alternative script, and preaching this text is to explore how the world is, if it is imagined through this alternative script.*

This thesis reminds us of two important recognitions. First, the biblical text is indeed a profound alternative to the text of the Enlightenment, and therefore an alternative to the dominant text with which most of us came to church. For a very long time we have assumed that the "American Dream," which is our version of Enlightenment freedom and well-being, coheres with the claims of the gospel.[30] It is the United States that is God's agent in the world, God's example, and God's most blessed people. I imagine that even those of us who reject blatant forms of this claim, in some lesser ways have been schooled effectively in the notion. Now we are coming to see, belatedly are required to see, that the American Dream as it is now understood has long since parted company with the claims of the gospel. Whereas the dominant text finds human initiative at the core of reality, the gospel witnesses to holiness as the core, and whereas it is Self that arises out of the hegemonic text, in the gospel it is the neighbor. The preacher and the congregation will be much liberated for serious preaching if it is understood that all of us, liberal and conservative, are in fact conducting an adjudication between these two competing texts, between which there is diminished overlap, and between which we do not want to choose. The preacher must show how this countertext of the gospel is a genuine alternative.

The second notion here is that the preacher, from this text, does not describe a gospel-governed world but helps the congregation imagine it.[31] Every text that describes and redescribes presents something that is not in hand, until the text is appropriated and all reality is passed through the text. Something like this must be the intent of Wallace Stevens in his enigmatic statement:

> Poetry is the supreme fiction, madame . . .
> But fictive things Wink as they will.[32]

The preacher traffics in a "fiction" that makes true. But that is why preaching is so urgent and must be done with such art. This world of the gospel is not "real," not available until this credible utterance authorizes a departure from a failed text and appropriation of this text.

Such an imaginative act of making fiction "real" is well exposited by Garrett Green in his assertion that "as" is the "copula of imagination."[33] I take Green to mean that an event or object must be interpreted "as" something before it becomes available. First, such a notion means that there are no available uninterpreted events or objects. They are beyond reach until interpreted, and when interpreted, they are seen or taken according to that "as."[34] Second, there is no right answer in the back of the book. Thus formally, any interpretive "as" has as much claim as any other. What the preacher then is doing is proposing that the world and our lives be seen or *taken as* under the aegis of the gospel. Such an imaginative "as" means a break with the world and our lives taken "as" under the aegis of Enlightenment construal. It is of course our usual assumption that the Enlightenment descriptions of reality are "given."[35] They are not, according to Green, given, but only a powerful, long-sustained "as," which is now to be countered by this evangelical "as."

10. *The proposal of this alternative script is not through large, comprehensive, universal claims, but through concrete, specific, local texts that in small ways provide alternative imagination.*

I have no doubt that every preacher and every interpreter of biblical texts operates with something like a "systematic theology."[36] Of course. But such systematic thinking, which is essential to some provisional coherence about reality, is not the primary mode of the biblical text. In fact, our macrovision in systematic theology is stitched together selectively from little texts that refuse long-term stabilization. Of course there is deep disagreement about this proposition. "Canonical criticism," as proposed by Brevard Childs, assumes long-term stabilization of a larger reading.[37] While there is some truth in that claim, it is equally (or more pertinently) true that continual study, reading, and reflection upon the text causes that stabilization to be constantly under review and change. Thus the insistence upon concrete, specific, local presentation is parallel to the nature of the text itself, which is composed of small parts, the precise relation of which to each other is not self-evident. The interpretive act is itself a major set of decisions about how the parts relate to each other this time.

Thus the preacher, if taking the text seriously, does not sound the whole of "biblical truth" in preaching but focuses on one detailed text to see what "as" it yields. It can be a great relief to the preacher not to have to utter a universal truth with each utterance, and it may be an assurance to the church that it is not given to pronounce universally on every issue that comes along.[38] It is enough to work with the local detail in the interest of transformation.

As examples of such "local work" we may cite almost any part of the Bible. We may note that in the powerful memories of Genesis 12—50, the action is quite local around one family, the members of which we are known by name and in considerable detail.[39] Perhaps more poignantly, the parables of Jesus focus remarkably on detail of one time and place.[40] Helpful dimensions of this accent on the concrete are offered by Sandra Schneiders in her programmatic use of the phrase "paschal imagination," in which she shows how the text moves beyond the subject/object split to world construal and construction.[41] And Jacob Neusner shows how very small acts of piety and ritual are ways in which practitioners can "imagine themselves to be Jews."[42] Such detail was perhaps not necessary when Christianity recently occupied a hegemonic position in our society, and one could deal in unnuanced summaries. Now, however, with the de-hegemonization of Christianity, we are back to the little pieces that in various ways make a claim against the dominant text. The preacher can understand the act of a single sermon as providing yet another detail to the very odd and different description of reality being enacted over time in the congregation.

11. *The work of preaching is an act of imagination, that is, an offer of an image through which perception, experience, and finally faith can be reorganized in alternative ways.*

The alternative voiced in textual preaching intends to show that this "scripting of reality" is in deep conflict with the dominant description of reality, so that the scripts are shown to be in tension with each other, if not in contradiction. If an alternative is not set forth with some clarity and vigor, then no choice is given, and no alternative choice is available. There is, of course, a long history of suspicion about imagination going clear back to Aristotle, suggesting that imagination is an inferior and unreliable source of knowledge.[43] With the failure of Enlightenment notions of "objectivity," imagination has made an important comeback as a mode of knowledge. Gaston Bachelard has exposited in powerful ways the creative function of imagination in the generation of knowledge.[44] Of his work, Richard Kearney writes that

> Bachelard . . . conceives of the imagination not as privation, but as audition—an acoustics of the *other* than self. His poetical model of imagination is two-dimensional: at once a giving and a taking, a projection and a discovery, a centrifugal exodus towards things and a centripetal return to the self. This notion of an "interlacing rhythm" which spans the breach between subjectivity and being epitomizes the Bachelardian theory of poetics.[45]

According to Bachelard, it is imagination that "valorizes" an alternative, and that, of course, is what preaching intends to do. Such a mode of preaching requires a break with our more usual mode of didactic, doctrinal, or moralistic preaching.

More recently, John Thiel has argued that imagination is a reliable mode of theological knowledge.[46] He, of course, knows that imagination is available for distortion, but asserts that it is no more available for distortion or less reliable for knowing than is "reason," a long-trusted practice in theological reflection.

It is thus my notion that the preacher and congregation can reconstrue the time and place of preaching as a time and place for the practice of imagination, that is, the reimagination of reality according to the evangelical script of the Bible. Such preaching does not aim at immediate outcomes but over time intends, detail by detail, to make a different world available in which different acts, attitudes, and policies are seen to be appropriate. To aim at this "underneath" dimension of faith is consistent with Ricoeur's conclusion that the "symbol gives rise to thought."[47] I would paraphrase Ricoeur to say that "the image gives rise to a new world of possibility"; preaching as understood here aims at images arising out of the text that may give rise to a church of new obedience.[48]

12. *Because old modes of certitude are no longer trusted, the preaching of these texts is not an offer of metaphysics but the enactment of a drama in which the congregation is audience but may at any point become participant.*

In *Texts Under Negotiation*, I have already articulated what I think is at issue in the move from metaphysical to dramatic thinking.[49] It is clear that dramatic modes of thought are more congenial to the way in which the Old Testament proceeds and in which the primal testimony of the New Testament is expressed. Characteristically, biblical faith may assume a metaphysic, but it is of little interest and value for the generation of faith. What counts, characteristically, is the dramatic turn of affairs to which the community bears witness and responds in praise, joy, and obedience. The result is that in the text itself, God is a character at play and at risk; in the preaching moment the congregation may see itself as among the characters in the drama.

The preacher, in the drama of the sermon, must thus "undo" much of the metaphysical preoccupation of the church tradition, to see whether the world can be imagined in terms of God's action in the ongoing account of the world, the nations, Israel, and the church. Such freedom and vitality as drama, which Hans Urs von Balthasar has shown to be definitive, is matched in yet another image offered by Frances Young.[50] Young proposes that the Bible is a musical score and that in each interpretive act, the score must be "performed" with the freedom and discipline always required of good performance. Moreover, Young proposes that much interpretation is a "cadenza" in the score, which gives the interpreter (here preacher) a good bit of room for maneuverability and idiosyncrasy.

13. *This dramatic rendering of imagination has as its quintessential mode narrative, the telling of a story, and the subsequent living of that story.*

The claim that narrative is a privileged mode in Christian preaching is of course not a new idea. After paying attention to the "testimony" of Israel and the early church, as in the earlier work of G. Ernest Wright, Reginald Fuller, and C. H. Dodd,[51] more recent study has considered the epistemological assumptions in the use of the genre of narrative. Such study has concluded that in this mode, reality itself has something of a narrative quality. Reality is an ongoing theater that has a plot of beginning, middle, and end and has characters who remain constant but also develop, change, and exercise great freedom.[52] As Dale Patrick has shown, God in the Bible narrative (as is Jesus in the New Testament) is an ongoing character who is endlessly rerendered and whom the preacher again rerenders.[53] The constancy of God is the constancy of a character in a narrative who must change in order to remain constant, and who necessarily violates our conventional notions of immutable transcendence.

Moreover, it is clear that the living of human life is embedded in a narrative rendering. Thus Hayden White has argued, persuasively in my judgment, that "history" is essentially a rhetorical activity in which past memory is "told" and "retold" in alternative ways, ways that may be intentional but that also take into account the vested interests of the narrating community.[54] And Alasdair MacIntyre has decisively shown that alternative ethical systems cannot be understood or assessed apart from the narrative world in which they are told, received, and valued.[55] Thus, narrative is not a secondary or auxiliary enterprise, but it is an act whereby social reality is constituted. Amos Wilder has championed the view long held by serious rhetoricians that speech, and specifically narrative speech, is constitutive of reality, so that narrative is indeed "world making."[56]

To be sure, there are many texts in the "script" of the Bible available to the preacher that are not narrative. Given my presuppositions, these are the most difficult to preach. It is my impression, nonetheless, that every text in any genre has something of a narrative behind it that generates it and through which the text is to be understood. Thus, for example, the Psalms are notoriously difficult preaching material. I suspect that the preacher characteristically either presents a narrative situation that is critically recoverable (as in Psalm 137), or imagines such a context that led this speaker to speak thusly. In the case of the Psalms, some of the superscriptions, even if not historically "reliable," provide a clue for such narrative construal.[57] And in the letters of Paul, a critically recoverable or homiletically imagined narrative context serves the preaching of the letters.

Such a mode of preaching has the spin-off effect of a drama being enacted, a story being narrated, and a plot being worked out. Such a mode holds the potential of showing the congregants that their lives (and life together) also constitute a drama being enacted and a story being told, in which they are characters with work to do, options to exercise, and loyalties to sustain or alter. This mode of preaching not only reconstrues the shape of the Bible but also reconstrues human life. It moves away from an essentialist focus to show that much of life is a rhetorical operation, and that we are indeed "speeched into newness."[58]

14. *The invitation of preaching (not unlike therapy) is to abandon the script in*

which one has had confidence and to enter a different script that imaginatively tells one's life differently.

The folk in the Bible are shown to be those who have often settled into a narrative that is deathly and destructive. Thus the early Hebrews had settled for a slave narrative as their proper self-presentation. That narrative is disrupted by another narrative that has Yahweh the liberator as the key and decisive agent. The decision to stay in Egypt or leave for the promise is a decision about which narrative to follow, whether to understand the "plot of life" according to the character Pharaoh or according to a different plot featuring Yahweh.[59] Mutatis mutandis, the New Testament narratives portray many folk either in a narrative of hopelessness and despair, or of self-righteousness and arrogance. In each case, they are invited into an alternative narrative, which is the narrative of the life-giving kingdom of God.

In *Texts Under Negotiation*, I have already suggested the analogue of psychotherapy.[60] I have no wish to "psychologize" preaching and only suggest an analogue. In such a parallel, I do not understand the conversation of psychotherapy as simply one of self-discovery, but I envision an active "therapist" who together with the one in need conducts a conversation in which an alternative account of his/her life may emerge. And if such an alternative narrative emerges, then the needful person in therapy has the opportunity and the task of adjudicating between the old narrative long since believed and the new narrative only now available. Such a person may eventually decide that the old narrative (from childhood) is not only destructive and paralyzing, but false, and a new one may be chosen that renarrates life in health. Many alternatives of one's life or the life of the world are made available in the process.

Mutatis mutandis, the task of the preacher is to exhibit this particular narrative script of the Bible, and to show how and in what ways life will be reimagined, redescribed, and relived if this narrative is embraced. The old-fashioned word for this process is "conversion." In my book *Biblical Perspectives on Evangelism*, I have shown in some detail what this might mean for the study and proclamation of the Bible.[61] It is in this context that Peter Berger understands the "social construction of reality" as a process of "switching worlds."[62] Nobody can "switch worlds" unless an alternative world is made richly available with great artistry, care, and boldness.

15. *The offer of an alternative script (to which we testify and bear witness as true) invites the listener out of his or her assumed context into many alternative contexts where different scripts may have a ring of authenticity and credibility.*

The "place" wherein I know myself to be living is not the only place where I could live. That is why it is important to pay attention to the several *contexts* of scripture that may be either critically recoverable or textually evoked. For example, I know myself to be living in a crime-threatened suburb in which I hear of the poor but on most days do not see them. In the text of Deuteronomy (to take one easy example), however, I do not listen in a threatened suburb. My "place" is different. The claimed location of this text is the River Jordan whereby "we" are about to enter the land of promise, a land filled with threatening Canaanite social structures and seductive Canaanite religion. As I listen I have important decisions to make, according to Deuteronomy, most concerning neighbors. Or alternatively, to take the critical judgment about Deuteronomy, I live in a seventh-century Jerusalem under the danger and threat of Assyria where the temptation is strong to accommodate and compromise until one's identity is gone.[63] In listening to this text, I can be at the Jordan or in Jerusalem only for a brief period, and then I return to the "reality" of suburbia. But being transported briefly by rhetoric invites me to resee and redescribe my own setting, perchance to act differently. Thus the hearing of a *counterscript* invites to a *countercontext* that over time may authorize and empower *counterlife*.

16. *Finally, I believe that the great pastoral fact among us that troubles everyone, liberal or conservative, is that the old givens of white, male, Western, colonial advantage no longer hold.*

The trust in those old givens takes many forms. It takes the form of power whereby we have known who was in charge, whom to trust and obey. It takes the form of knowledge, for we could identify the knowing authorities who had a right to govern. It takes the form of certitude, because the world was reliably and stably ordered. And those in control or authority had great finesse in conducting the kind of "hegemonic theatre" that kept the world closely ordered and coherent.[64]

No special argument needs to be made about the demise of that world, even though a lot of political and ecclesiastical mileage is available out of the claim that the old world can be sustained even longer. The demise of that hegemony touches us in many different ways, personal and public, but there is in any case a widely shared sense that things are "out of control." It is, I submit, widely shared not only by beneficiaries of the old patterns of certitude, but also by many of its perceived victims. Nothing seems to be reliable as it used to be. And that sense of "out of control" invites all kinds of extreme notions of fear and anxiety that eventuate in acts and policies of brutality.

In that context, preachers are entrusted with a text, alternative to the failed text of white, male, Western hegemony, which mediates and valorizes a viable world outside that given, privileged advantage of certitude and domination. It turns out that the script we have trusted in the Enlightenment is an unreliable script, even though we have been massively committed to it. And now, we are wondering, is there a more adequate script out of which we may reimagine our lives? Almost no one would articulate coming to worship on such grounds. Nonetheless, I believe there is a haunting wonderment if there is a text (and an interpreter) that can say something that will "make sense" out of our pervasive nonsense.[65] It is my conviction that neither old liberal ideologies, old conservative certitudes, nor critical claims made for the Bible will now do. Our circumstance permits and requires the preacher to do something we have not been permitted or required to do before. It is an awesome risk to see if this text, with all of our interpretive inclinations, can voice and offer reality in a redescribed way that is credible and evocative of a new humanness, rooted in holiness and practiced in neighborliness.

4

Testimony as a
Decentered Mode of Preaching

A *radically resituated* church requires preaching to be cast in an entirely *different mode and genre*. For a very long time Christian preaching has been in a *hegemonic church*, that is, a church that participated in and was allied with dominant forms of social, cultural, economic, and intellectual life. This participation and alliance meant that the church could get by with making claims of certainty and that the church had to accept responsibility for certitudes in relation to and in support of the hegemony.

Specifically, the socioeconomic hegemony required certain intellectual-ideological certitudes as a legitimation of power. The church was in the business of certitudes, and its preaching was necessarily cast in *genres of certitude*. We may in broad sweep identify three facets of that theological-homiletical practice of certitude:

1. *The Constantinian establishment* of Christianity made Christianity—and its preaching—an ally of imperial power and a speaker of certitudes that were to serve the large claims of the empire. The bishops who finally settled the creedal foundations of the dogmatic tradition were much associated with the vagaries of imperial power and domination.

2. *The catholic synthesis* of faith was rooted in those old ecumenical agreements and creedal formulations and received classical articulation in the high Middle Ages, when the popes were large political brokers and the great medieval theologians provided an ideational coherence that sustained and justified the intellectual-moral understandings of Europe. Not only was there no salvation outside the church, there was no thinking outside the church. And so the refutation of Islam, the defeat of the infidels in the Crusades, and the expulsion of Islam from Spain all contributed to the totalizing claims of the church. (We do not need, moreover, to comment upon the role of marginality assigned to Jews as a part of the same totalization.)

3. *The Reformation* and the subsequent Thirty Years' War did indeed

disrupt the uniform and coherent claims of Christendom at a political level, for now there was a great political divide out of the war, and there were two competing engines of interpretation.[1] None of that, however, challenged Christian hegemony in any important way. Reformation and Counter-Reformation thinking were equally within the environs of Christendom, and both understood that they were making absolute claims, even if neighbors across the Rhine were making different, even contradictory absolute claims.

4. The unquestioned claims of Christendom were decisively challenged in the rise of *Enlightenment rationality,* an intellectual movement associated especially with Francis Bacon and René Descartes and culminating in Immanuel Kant and Georg Wilhelm Hegel.[2] There is no doubt that the Enlightenment aimed at emancipation of truth from Christian interpretive authority. And yet it seems fair to insist that even the Enlightenment was a European affair that operated within the confines of Christendom and continued to make absolutist, universal claims that were uncritically Euro-contexted. While the theological claims of Christianity were deeply under assault, the cultural hegemony of intellectual-ideological Europe persisted without challenge.

a. What came to be "liberal Christianity" (Albrecht Ritschl, Adolf Harnack) practiced Enlightenment rationality and dealt with "universal truth" that reflected "the spirit of the age." It is clear in retrospect that the function, if not the intention, of historical criticism, was to make the Bible congenial to Enlightenment rationality, so that the particularity of the Bible was made to fit Enlightenment universals.

b. The extreme reaction to "liberal Christianity," which came to be expressed as fundamentalism, was not basically different. The sort of certitudes it offered were in their formulation and mode of argument quite congenial to Enlightenment rationality. Thus in terms of hegemonic certitude, liberal Christianity and fundamentalist Christianity are twins, both claiming universal scope for their particularized certitudes. Thus I should suggest an important intellectual-ideational continuity from the Constantinian establishment of the church, through its grand medieval articulation (and in its protesting alternative in the Reformation), and into Enlightenment rationality that produced both liberal and fundamentalist articulations. Indeed, I should suggest that the founding of the World Council of Churches in 1948, as a great act of postwar courage, was an ecumenical venture in its time completely marked by Euro-American hegemony.

5. Now if this analysis is correct, then I suggest that the preaching of the church has had a terrible burden of large, universal truths befitting the certitudes on which the hegemony relied. I observe two simple facets of such preaching:

a. It was cast in the articulation of propositions, that is, ideas that made a claim of universal credence. Propositional preaching stems from, as well as aims at, certitude.[3]
b. The three-point sermon is rooted in the evangelical structure of Luther's catechism, so that it has an intense theological basis, but even the three classic points are profoundly hegemonic:
    i.   The problem is universal.
    ii. The solution is clear and everywhere known.
    iii. The new possibility is everywhere available.

One departed from such a sermon with certitude, not only personally and locally reassured, but confidently reassured for all the others, everywhere.[4] Given the history of Christendom, I think it could not have been otherwise. It is possible to say that such preaching is arrogant, but I prefer to observe how remarkably demanding it is, demanding in its moral courage and demanding in its intellectual requirements. And as we all know who preach, demanding in its implicit political duty.

The Decentered Church

Hegemonic modes of preaching are no longer possible or required in a decentered church. It is evident, I take it, that the church is no longer part of the intellectual-ideational hegemony of our culture, for reasons that are complex and partly obscure. Indeed, one can say that hegemonic power itself is in some disarray. However, the church has become (in both the United States and in Europe) profoundly disestablished and decentered, so that it is no longer able to voice the kinds of certitudes that will sustain the hegemony, and increasingly, elements of the church are no longer willing even to try. In very large sweep, we may say that the church is now faced with a radically *secularized* society, in which the old assumptions of Christendom no longer prevail or command widespread and almost automatic acceptance. It is not possible or important, for our purposes, to try to understand how this has come about. But it is possible to say that as the church has colluded with the old economic, political hegemony, that is, the *ancien régime*, it was poorly situated to respond to the new cultural, intellectual situation that displaced that *ancien régime*.

In any case, at a quite practical level, the church is no longer a dominant intellectual force in society and no longer can count on cultural reenforcement. The practical signs of that situation include the worry about numbers and dollars in the church, the loss of force in the office of the pastor, and the awareness that our foundational claims of faith are increasingly in deep tension with the dominant visions of the day. The mainline churches have become sidelined, and I shall argue that this new circumstance both requires and permits a fresh casting of preaching.[5]

As long ago as Luther, it was suggested that the church lived in a "Babylonian Captivity."[6] By this phrase, Luther referred to the fact that the gospel had been captured by the Roman Catholic sacramental system that he viewed as fundamentally hostile to the gospel. That is, the gospel was in an alien environment that denied the gospel its true force and certainly denied the gospel any privileged hearing. Since the time of Luther, the image of "Babylonian exile" has been used to situate the gospel—or the church—in a secular environment that, if not hostile, is at least indifferent to the gospel.

The metaphor of Babylonian exile will serve well for my urging. It is my sense that when the preacher proclaims in the baptized community in our present social context, the preacher speaks to *a company of exiles.*[7] This does not mean that the exiles will be all weak, powerless, inept people, for many are formidable. Nor does it mean that they are intellectually inferior, for some may be enormously astute, discerning, and sophisticated. It means simply that such people are at work seeking to maintain an *alternative identity*, an *alternative vision* of the world, and an *alternative vocation* in a societal context where the main forces of culture seek to deny, discredit, or disregard that odd identity. The great problem for exiles is cultural assimilation. The primary threat to those ancient Jews was that members of the community would decide that Jewishness is too demanding, or too dangerous, or too costly, and simply accept Babylonian definitions and modes of reality. And surely Jews in exile worried that their young would see no point in the hassle of being Jewish. And so it has been with Jews in all their long history of displacement—which is what makes the state of Israel so poignant—the only place where a Jew is not in a hostile, dissonant environment.

For Christians, however, to stand now—like Jews—in a culture that dismisses, disregards, and derides odd identity is a new venture in the West, at least since Constantine. We ourselves, moreover, know about the decision that Christian baptism is too demanding, too dangerous, too costly. We ourselves surely know, moreover, about the next generation that too readily decides that discipleship is not worth it. As Jews disappeared into the woodwork of Babylon, so Christians now, as never before in the West, disappear into the hegemony of secularism. And for those who resist the invitation to secularism, the sustenance of Christian-baptismal identity is indeed an intentional act that requires discipline, support, and practice. This crisis of course helps us to understand the compulsion to coercive authoritarianism and moralistic maintenance of Christian identity, except that people like us believe that such coercion for the sake of the gospel is contradictory and will

not work. Our task is to see about alternative practices, disciplines, and intentions that may sustain an alternative, subversive, countercultural identity.

Preaching for Exiles

The needs, possibilities, and satisfactions for Christians in exile are very
different from those in a season of hegemony. The exiles are not required
to sustain the empire. Exiles are not required to spout universal truths that
will withstand scrutiny everywhere in the empire. Thus what passes for
proclamation among exiles is more effective when it is more modest, more
local, and more subversive. I will suggest three facets of proclamation that
seem to me thoroughly biblical and completely pertinent to every generation of exiles.

1. Among exiles, it is not necessary or even preferable to engage
in *monolithic* language, that is, language that is one-dimensional,
excessively flat, too sure, too serious, with too much closure. Monolithic
language that smacks of closure is too much an echo of the rhetoric of the
empire, precisely what is to be gotten away from. Whereas the empire
needs certitude, exiles need space, room for maneuver, breathing
opportunities that allow for negotiation, adjudication, ambiguity, and
playfulness.

Thus, for example, I was told that during the terror of apartheid in
South Africa, Old Testament scholars were not allowed to say of the book
of Jonah that it might be fiction, that it might be satire, or irony, or humor.
Interpretation needed to be flat, one-dimensional, and on the surface, in
order to suggest that there is no slippage in the Bible, that is, no ground
for slippage in social relations.

In contrast to members of the hegemony, exiles live all day, every day
in the world of imperial closure, certitude, and reductionism. The exile
does not need more of this in church, but requires relief from such
oppressive closeness that is common both in economic and in interpretive
practice. The playfulness permitted in proclamation to exiles is well
articulated in much African American preaching that is teasing, mocking,
satirical, and repetitious, acts that imagine and conjure free space to which
"whitey" has no great access.

2. Proclamation to exiles must be intensely *Yahweh-focused*, that is,
preoccupied with the character of Yahweh as a *credible, normal, and indis-*
pensable character in the world that is imagined among exiles and available
for their lives. Exiles have already concluded that the imperial gods are
hostile to them, or at least indifferent to their plight, so that there will not
ever be help from that quarter. Thus speech that revolves around established,
settled gods is a negative for discerning exiles. Exiles want to know if there
is yet another rendering of reality that has at its center a different Character

who will be neither indifferent nor hostile, a God who is able and willing to make a difference in the lives of exiles, which now seem futile and hopeless.

> The rendering of Yahweh among exiles must be *credible*, that is, linked to real life circumstance.
>
> The rendering of Yahweh must be *normal*. Yahweh is not some supernatural oddity that needs explanation, but an accepted, assumed, embraced Character who belongs invariably and without question in the middle of the narrative.
>
> The rendering of Yahweh must be *indispensable*. The tale of existence offered exiles must be told so that Yahweh is seen to be a necessary character, not an extra or an addendum. If one omits Yahweh from the tale, the tale collapses into nonsense. Among the exiles, it is important that Yahweh be a real and key player in their existence.

3. Proclamation to exiles must be the rendering of a script that is *not controlled by, contaminated by, or intruded upon by the hegemonic power* of the empire. The exilic community requires a scripting of reality that is not subordinated to the rationality of the empire. It is—of course—my urging that the Bible is such a script that can be rendered among exiles, but it must be a script not subordinated to either (a) Enlightenment rationality (as in historical criticism) or (b) scholastic dogmatic tradition, both of which are attempts to tame and domesticate this irascible reality of Yahweh.

When the Bible is seen as an unadministered script for exiles, it is clear that this script meets the first two conditions for proclamation among exiles:

a. It is deeply saturated with Yahweh.
b. The Yahweh in the script is not given in monolithic language but in playful, venturesome, teasing, ambiguous language.

The convergence of *Yahweh* and *open language* creates rhetorical/ imaginative/theological space in which exiles can live their lives freely, so that the empire cannot rob them of identity, that is, cannot crush or over-whelm their baptismal identity.

The upshot of such a scripting of reality is an evangelical imagination marked by the following:[8]

> *Hyperbole*, wonderful overstatements of both hurt and possibil-ity that are not curbed by the sober rationality of the hege-mony.

Irony, statements that characteristically say something other and something more than they appear to say, so that the empire can never quite detect the danger and the threat that are under way in such utterance, because only the "clued-in" can decode. Examples of such ironic speech may include the narrative of 1 Samuel 16:1–13, the interplay of Daniel and Nebuchadnezzar in Daniel 4, and the general disruption of the royal narrative of 1 and 2 Kings caused by the unsettling intrusion of the prophets.

Contradiction, such as that stated in Exodus 34:6–7 in the inner life and inclination of Yahweh.

Deliberate ambiguity, as in the obscure identity of the adversary in the drama of Genesis 32:22–32.

In all of these cases, the text is not nearly as straightforward and accessible as our hegemonic interpretation wants to make it. Such rhetoric as is appropriate among exiles deabsolutizes the givens and the certitudes of the empire, makes life not so settled or closed or sure or controllable as it seemed to be, and maintains Yahweh as a key, free player in the process of subversion. Such proclamation has no interest in spouting *certitudes*, for its work is the modest process of creating *openings* and *breathing places* for those who do not live at the center of power, certitude, or privilege. This is indeed hazardous rhetoric for those who live hazardous lives. And if the forces of the empire ever detect what is being said or being generated by such speech, they would recognize that such speech is indeed "hazardous to their health."

Testifying to New Reality

Now with that long introduction, I wish to propose that *the rhetorical practice among exiles given in scripture is best understood as testimony*, that is, utterance by alleged first-person witnesses who offer an account of experience that depends solely upon the trustworthiness of the witnesses, but that cannot appeal for verification either to agreed-upon *metaphysics* or to external *historical data*. It is, rather, originary of new reality that was not available until uttered. The testimony uttered among exiles can appeal to no answer in the back of the book, but must make its own case as best it can. The reason that appeal to metaphysics or external historical data or answer in the back of the book is not possible, moreover, is that all such appeals refer back to imperial reality and imperial rationality. It is the intention of testimony among exiles to live outside that territory, and so appeal cannot be made to those kinds of verification. Such testimony, moreover, intends to attest to a version of reality that subverts accepted, given accounts of reality upon which the hegemony relies. The initial effect of such testimony is to make one uneasy with the "assured claims" of the hegemonic certitudes. But beyond that initial uneasiness, such testimony, if accepted as true, may indeed conjure an alternative world that permits alternative, lived possibilities.

This notion of testimony has something in it of the religious "testifying" of Baptists who tell in the congregation about the evidence for God in their own lives. But I have reference to a different image, namely, a court of law before which Israel is to stand to give its testimony about the reality of Yahweh. In the end, what the court—that is, *the exilic community* itself, or more largely, *the observing empire* or *the belatedly reading, interpreting community*—has of Yahweh is nothing more and nothing less than what this testimony provides. *Yahweh is a product and consequence of Israel's testimony.* What happens in the Bible, and in the community that continues to attend to the Bible (of which the preacher is the most recent member), is a chain of witnesses, in which subsequent witnesses repeat and reiterate and interpret and extrapolate from what earlier witnesses have said. The preachers are the last in a long line of witnesses, all of whom are dependent upon the primary witnesses, but who are also dependent upon every generation of witnesses in the chain. Witnesses of course always fall short of proof. They only seek to make a credible case and to offer a case that is more credible and more compelling than the case offered by other witnesses. The witnesses hope to convince the court that this is a credible account of how the world is. And what a "case" consists of is some data, carefully framed in a coherent narrative, with much of the "connecting" material around the data being supplied by the strategy of the attorneys and the shrewdness of the witnesses.

I shall argue that in the end, most generally, all of the Bible is testimony of a new construal of reality, which lives outside imperial rationality and which cannot and does not appeal either to historical data or consensus metaphysics or answers in the back of the book.[9] But before I make such a large, generalizing claim, I want to look specifically at practices of witnesses and testimony in the texts that form the primary ground for my thesis.

1. If we are to think of testimony by and for and among exiles, then the place to begin is in II Isaiah, the primal exilic document of the Old Testament. The pastoral agenda in II Isaiah is *homecoming for exiles*. But the theological issue is whether *the God who wills homecoming* is stronger than *the Babylonian gods who will exile*. And so the pastoral issue of historical possibility comes down to a theological issue of who is *true God*. It was easier for the exiles, as it always is for the marginated, to accept the hegemonic gods of Babylonia and to stay in their despairing exile. They are, however, here summoned otherwise. I suggest, then, that at the core of II Isaiah is the activity of

testimony that asserts that Yahweh is stronger and more trustworthy than the Babylonian gods. As a consequence, this testimony summons the exiles to bear witness to Yahweh against the gods of Babylon, and thereby to defeat and depart from their own despair, and so to reject their excuse for remaining in exile.

We may distinguish two practices of testimony in II Isaiah. First, there is *testimony to Israel*, for which I will cite two pivotal texts: Isaiah 40:1–11 and Isaiah 52:7. Isaiah 40:1–11 presents Yahweh speaking in Yahweh's heavenly government, deciding the new decree of heaven that will turn the reality of earth and that will emancipate the Jews from their bondage.[10] The text culminates in a poetic mandate, presumably to a member of the heavenly court:

> Get you up to a high mountain,
>   O Zion, herald of good tidings;
> Lift up your voice with strength,
>   O Jerusalem, herald of good tidings, . . .
> say to the cities of Judah,
>   "Behold your God."
>
> (Isa. 40:9)

This is a piece of poetry, not history, not doctrine, not ontology. It is invitational poetry, invitation to an alternative perception of reality. And because it is poetry, the references are not very precise. The messenger to announce the heavenly decree is Zion or Jerusalem. But what interests us in the text is twofold:

a. The "herald of good tidings" is the messenger of *gospel*, that is, the carrier of the news. The text uses, for the first time in Israel, the technical term "to announce the gospel" (*bāśar*). This is news of a new reality in the world, a reality not known or available until this utterance.

b. The substance of "the gospel" is "Behold your God." It is a dramatic, venturesome oral exhibit of the God of Israel who had been mute and absent and seemingly impotent, but is now visible, engaged, and triumphant. The news is that Yahweh has not been eliminated by Babylon, as the evidence of the empire had seemed to suggest. But notice, it is a messenger, conjured by a poet, who gives evidence at the behest of Yahweh's heavenly government about the Decisive Agent in the life of Israel, an agent from whom the exiles had expected nothing and from whom Babylon had feared nothing. Inside this new construal of reality, the exiles may now expect and the Babylonians had better fear.

> How beautiful upon the mountains
>   are the feet of him who brings good tidings,
> who publishes peace,

> who brings good tidings of good
> who publishes salvation,
> who says to Zion, "Your God reigns."
>
> (Isa. 52:7)

Again, "good tidings" is the technical term for "gospel" (*bāśar*), the term first mobilized by this poet. Here it is not Zion as messenger, but messenger sent to Zion. The poet conjures a breathless runner come from Babylon to report to the exiles in their hopelessness and helplessness that a battle has been fought and Yahweh has won and taken power: "Your God rules!" Your God has just become king! Your God has prevailed! The gods of the empire have been defeated.

The result is that the Jews are now free to go home. The news is theological, but it is world-changing, with both a permit and a requirement implied. Note well, that if the Jews go home, it will be because they accept the world that is available to them only on the lips of this messenger, who in turn is available to them only in the utterance of the poet who provides the messenger within the poem. The poet, Second Isaiah, is creating a credible account of reality in which Yahweh is a normal and indispensable character. The poet bids that the exiles should assent to this version of reality, a subversion, and disengage from the dominant version of reality fostered by Babylon. Change verdicts, change narratives, and so enact an alternative existence!

The exiles, however, are not only *addressed* by such gospel testimony that makes available a new world. They are also *summoned to testimony* and assigned their own dangerous roles as witnesses in court. We may notice three texts in which this role is assigned to the exiles: Isaiah 43:8–13; 44:8; and Isaiah 48:6, 20–21.

In Isaiah 43:8–13 the issue is joined between "true witnesses" and "other witnesses" who clearly are not telling the truth. To be sure, the issue is a theological contest between gods. But everything for *the gods* depends upon *the witnesses*. Thus theological truth follows faithful utterance:

> Let them [the other gods] bring their witnesses to justify (*ṣādaq*) them,
>   and let them hear and say, "It is true" (*'emeth*).
> You are my witnesses, says the LORD.
>
> (Isa. 43:9–10)

In verses 11–12a, there is a doxological declaration of Yahweh in Yahweh's own mouth. Midst that self-assertion of Yahweh is this statement in verse 12b: "You are my witnesses." Everything depends upon witnesses, upon compelling testimony, in order to win the assent of the watching court. The truth of God rides on the testimony of the witnesses. The exilic witnesses in Israel are summoned, moreover, to give an account of reality to the court that flies in the face of the formidable evidence offered by the hegemony. The testimony of the exiles is indeed an alternative counter-version of reality.

> Fear not, be not afraid;
>> have I not told you of old and declared it?
>> And you are my witnesses,
> Is there a God besides me?
>> There is no rock; I know not any.
>> > (Isa. 44:8)

In Isaiah 44:8 the debate is about God. Yahweh tells the exilic witnesses what to say: "I am the only one." And Israel is to assert that claim as fact. God says to God's people, "You go give evidence, assert that I am the only one." That assignment is risky in the empire. It is for that reason that the mandating God says to the witnesses, "Fear not!" Why "Fear not"? Because the witnesses are about to give evidence that contradicts the dominant truth of the empire. Such testimony is intrinsically fearful. But beyond that, the Babylonians will never tolerate such testimony and, so far as we know, Yahweh has no program of "protected witnesses." Notice that in 44:9, there is reference to the witnesses for the idols who "neither see nor know." Those gods are big, phony nothings. And so are their witnesses! That negative dismissal of the other gods and their witnesses is offered as assurance for the risk that the exilic witnesses are summoned to run for their odd version of the truth.

> You have heard; now see all this;
>> and will you not declare it? . . .
>> declare this with a shout of joy, proclaim it,
> send it forth to the end of the earth;
>> say: "Yahweh has redeemed his servant Jacob!"
>> > (Isa. 48:6, 20)

In Isaiah 48:6, 20, the exiles are to give an out-loud account of their own experience of Yahweh's startling, decisive, transformative emergence in their life. Their work—for themselves and for others—is to provide first-person evidence of a credible, alternative construal of reality. This text makes unmistakably clear how much depends upon faithful, courageous utterance that defies the established utterance of the empire. This testimony intends to contradict and challenge other evidence, and to force the court to reconsider its heretofore settled assumption about the truth.

In other texts, such as Isaiah 41:21–29 and 45:20–21, the poetry is set up as a court contest, in which each god gives evidence of god-ship, and each god mobilizes adherents to give account of "his" truth. Yahweh is the marginated, exiled God among Jewish exiles. The weight of public opinion is against Yahweh and against Israel, as it is always against exiles. But this community, given its summons, mandate, and conviction, keeps at its countertestimony. Everything for its own life in the world depends upon this utterance. And in larger scope, these witnesses do not doubt that everything, even for the empire, depends upon heeding and embracing this account of reality.

2. Second Isaiah is the showcase example of testimony as a mode of faith in the Old Testament. But II Isaiah did not happen de novo. Isaiah 52:7, the key text of gospel testimony, centers in the assertion, "Your God reigns." It is most plausible that the poet of 52:7 lifted that assertion verbatim from an older, long-practiced liturgical formula. In Psalm 96:10, a psalm that surely belongs to the period of the Solomonic temple, Israel sings, Say among the nations, "Your God reigns." The claim is the same as in Isaiah 52:7 addressed to Zion in the same phrasing. In the psalm, however, the claim is to be asserted by Israel to the nations. The purpose of the assertion is to give testimony that Yahweh's governance is operative, and all, everywhere, must take it into serious account. Earlier in this typical liturgical piece, moreover, Israel utilizes six verbs of assertion: "sing, sing, sing, bless, tell, declare" (vv. 1–3). The fifth verb, "tell," is the term *bāśar*, "gospel." Thus " 'gospel' Yahweh's salvation from day to day to the nations." The substance of that news announced to the nations is that Yahweh has become king, that is, has defeated the oppressive, displacing gods of the empire, and by derivation, the oppressive, displacing powers of the world. The powers of the world are now to conclude that they are no longer empowered or legitimated in their anti-Yahweh policies because their gods no longer have the authority to legitimate.

The liturgy invites Israel to witness to evidence from its own life, and thereby to construct an alternative account of reality in which Yahweh is credible, normal, and indispensable. The testimony is aimed first of all at the people in the liturgy, that is, the Israelites. But the testimony characteristically moves beyond those present in the proclamation and intends to address those outside the community who must also reckon with this Character who comes to power in, with, and under the testimony of Israel.

3. We may for a moment push not only behind the dramatic movement of II Isaiah and the exile, but also behind and outside the great liturgical enterprise of the temple of Solomon as reflected in the enthronement psalms. Here I shall cite three examples (Judges 5:10–11; 1 Samuel 12:3–18; and Micah 6:1–5) of testimony that appear to me to be elemental and definitional in Israel. The three texts have in common that they all

speak of Yahweh's mighty deeds (*sidqot*), which constitute the substance of
the gospel. That is, each space of the decisive way in which this
Character—credible, normal, and indispensable—has made a decisive
difference in the life and world of Israel.

> Tell of it, you who ride on tawny asses,
>> you who sit on rich carpets,
>> and you who walk by the way.
> To the sound of musicians at the watering places,
>> there they repeat the triumphs of Yahweh,
>> the *triumphs* of his peasantry in Israel.
>
> (Judg. 5:10–11)

These verses are in the old Song of Deborah, thus a model of Israel's
earliest self-awareness as being linked to this odd God. They invite *a
conversation of saturation* that continues while riding, sitting, and walking,
that is, all the time.[11] There is to be much talking and telling and narrating and bearing witness. The talk is to happen at the watering places, at the
oases, at the village wells, while the community does its most mundane,
daily routines, where the women gather to gossip, to sing while the buskers
play and entertain and enjoy.

In that context, Israel is to talk endlessly about Yahweh, about Yahweh's
victories, about Yahweh's acts of making things right, about Yahweh's
solidarity with the peasants who, without Yahweh, are hopeless and
helpless. Israel is to repeat these exhibits of Yahweh: "Sing them over again
to me. . . ." Do so in order to inculcate and socialize the children. But do
so as well to keep up your own nerve, to sustain your odd identity and your
commitment to this odd God.

I thought the subject was "the triumphs of Yahweh," the mighty deeds
of God in history. Yes, it is. Except those deeds are also "the triumphs of
his peasantry." Thus the singing and telling is about the acts of courage
whereby Yahweh's people have run risks for an alternative life in the world.
But this is not dogmatic theology. And so the poetic parallels can sing of
Yahweh's actions and the deeds of the peasants, for it is all the same. Say,
say it again, repeat it, and in so doing make a world with Yahweh as credible,
normal and indispensable. This is not a courtroom, but it is nonetheless a
context in which competing versions of reality are in play against each
other. And those who speak while they ride and sit and walk are advocates
for a particular, peculiar Yahweh-world.

First Samuel 12:3–18 is Samuel's farewell address. He is presented as a
tired, old man, under deep criticism from his constituency. In response to
criticism, he defends himself and seeks honorable retirement and vindication
for his long season of leadership. He defies the community and asks what
he has done wrong. He introduces the rhetoric of litigation: "Testify

against me."[12] Of course, they cannot, for there is no such evidence, as the text insists. And then Samuel testifies against them. His testimony has an odd character, because what he does is give an account of Yahweh with whom he is closely identified. He sets up the dispute so that a vindication of Yahweh is in effect also his own vindication. What Samuel recites are Yahweh's "saving deeds" that extend from Jacob (v. 8) through the judges, and finally to the kingship (v. 13). He recites the entire history of Israel, in order to show that the key player in the whole enterprise is the completely reliable Yahweh who is beyond challenge.

Of course, the Israelites who listen cannot refute him, given the grounds of the assertion. So the narrative concludes, "The people greatly feared the LORD and Samuel" (v. 18). That is, Samuel had won the dispute and was vindicated along with Yahweh. But note, the entire matter is one of rhetoric. Samuel is a rhetorical player who forms a narrative world for Israel with Yahweh at its center. And in so doing, Samuel forcibly prohibits any other account of reality. He precludes any account of reality which does not center in Yahweh. And by implication, he precludes a world which does not have Samuel himself as the key human player. He evokes assent from Israel, because the community lives in that narrative world, that is, regards his testimony as true. Given that narrative construal of reality, Israel can entertain no alternative.

Micah 6:1–5 is articulated in juridical language with a disputatious, partisan presentation of evidence.

> Hear what the LORD says:
>   Rise, *plead your case* before the mountains,
>   and let hills hear your voice.
> Hear, you mountains, the *controversy* of the LORD,
>   and you enduring foundations of the earth;
> for the LORD has a *controversy* with his people,
>   and he will *contend* with Israel.
> "O my people, what have I done to you?
>   In what have I wearied you? Answer me!
> For I brought you up from the land of Egypt . . .
>   that you may know the saving acts of Yahweh."

Like 1 Samuel 12, this text is disputatious, cast in juridical form. In 1 Samuel 12, the adjudication of truth is between Samuel and his contemporaries. Here it is between Yahweh and Israel. In both cases, what is in dispute is the truth, that is, the reliability of Yahweh (and in the one case the reliability of Samuel). In both cases, what is true about Yahweh depends upon persuasive utterance. The Micah assertion provides evidence that Yahweh is indeed a reliable provider, sustainer, and deliverer to whom Israel owes obedience that takes the form of mercy and justice. As in the

Samuel passage, there is no response from the listeners who are Samuel's adversaries. We are left to conclude that the rhetorical claim for Yahweh is so decisive that any adversary can only remain silent, clearly defeated and without a compelling rival claim for truth.

All three of these texts—Judges 5:10–11; 1 Samuel 12:3–18; Micah 6:1–5—make assertions about Yahweh's *sidqot*. In Judges 5, it is a peasant assertion of what is true and seemingly not contested in the community of telling. In the other two texts, it is testimony in dispute, but testimony that permits no answer that would propose an alternative truth. In all three cases it is the *telling* that yields *reality* when the witness is believed. In all three texts, the testimony seeks to establish a claim not supported by any hegemonic force but dependent solely upon the power of testimony that counters the anti-Yahweh claims of the hegemony.

4. As a last example of truth enacted as testimony in a community of the marginated, I turn to the great prayer of Ezra in Nehemiah 9, a prayer that entails testimony at the end of the Old Testament period. To be sure, this public act of prayer is of a very different sort from the texts we have just mentioned. It is addressed to Yahweh and to no one else. It culminates in verse 38 (= Heb. 10:1) in a communal covenant. Nonetheless, its force is testimonial. Its dialectical theme is *Israel's sin* and *Yahweh's mercy*. At least ostensibly, the prayer testifies to Yahweh about Yahweh's characteristic and appropriate activity, which is forgiveness for Israel:

> But you are a God ready to forgive, gracious and merciful, slow to anger and abounding in steadfast love, and you did not forsake them. (Neh. 9:17)
> You in your great mercies did not forsake them. (v. 19)
> According to your great mercies you gave them saviors. (v. 27)
> Many times you rescued them according to your great mercies. (v. 28)
> Nevertheless, in your great mercies you did not make an end of them or forsake them, for you are a gracious and merciful God. (v. 31)
> Now therefore, our God—the great and mighty and awesome God, keeping covenant and steadfast love—do not treat lightly all the hardship that has come upon us. . . . Here we are, slaves to this day . . . we are in great distress. (vv. 32–37)

It is remarkable that at the end of the prayer (vv. 32–37), there is no positive petition. There is only, "Do not treat lightly all the hardship." Moreover, it is remarkable that the prayer culminates in verse 38 with covenant. This ending suggests to me that while the prayer seeks to instruct Yahweh in Yahweh's proper action, that is, bears witness, at the same time the prayer surely has a didactic function. It evokes a covenant in Israel. The prayer testifies to Israel about the *character of Yahweh*, and the consequent *character of Israel*; that is, Yahweh is merciful, and therefore Israel is obedient.

I submit that this prayer is not unlike the Great Eucharistic prayer of the church, a prayer concerning "prophets and apostles, martyrs and saints." It is surely a "real prayer" addressed to God. It is equally sure that the prayer has a didactic, nurturing intention, designed to situate Israel and to give Israel its particular identity, that is, to give the church its baptismal identity. The prayer contends for and evokes one embraced reality rather than any other.

The Testimony of Exiles

This twofold function of the prayer of Ezra as *witness to Yahweh* and *witness to Israel* brings me to my final point, namely, the intention *of Israel's testimony*. I submit that Israel's testimony concerning Yahweh characteristically has a twofold intention.

1. First, it explicitly and unmistakably is addressed to the community of exiles. The twin temptations of exile are *despair and assimilation*, both temptations to give up a peculiar identity for a less-demanding, less-risky identity. The purpose of this testimony is to state and reenforce the exilic community in a particular identity, in a plot that has a specific Yahweh as its key character. It is this plot that resists despair and that allows Israel to refuse assimilation. The socialization process surely creates a network of social relations that hold a person in this framework of dense identity.

But the explicit claim of the testimony is not sociological. It is theological. It is linkage to the God who *saves and commands* that is the burden of the testimony.[13] It is this testimony, judged to be true, that gives Israel its habitat in the world. That is, in testimony the exilic community speaks to itself, tells its Yahwistic truth to itself so that it may maintain its freedom and distance from the hegemony. "Knowing Yahweh" means engaging a world of joy and well-being outside the hegemony that is alien to Yahweh, that is committed to alien gods who have no power to give either joy or well-being.

2. In this testimony, Israel is not a sect. It does not withdraw into its own life. It is always a community of exiles intensely aware of the hegemonic community with which it lives in tension. Thus in Jeremiah 29:7 Israel is enjoined to pray for Babylon because upon the peace of Babylon depends its own peace. Israel is not offered any "separate peace" by Yahweh. Thus in a less intense and sustained way, Israel's testimony addresses the hegemony, insisting that the truth of Yahweh given in the testimony is a truth that must needs concern the hegemony.

In Isaiah 52:7, it is "*Say to Zion*, 'Your God reigns.' " But in Psalm 96:10, quoted by Isaiah 52:7, it is "*Say among the nations*, 'The LORD is king.' "

What matters decisively among the exiles is also known to matter decisively to the nations who are addressed by the testimony. The same testimony that vivifies Israel also requires the nations to decide about the truthfulness of Yahweh as given in the testimony. The following cases indicate a secondary address "to the nations."[14]

a. In Exodus 5:1–2, Pharaoh is commanded by Yahweh to "let my people go." Pharaoh responds, "Who is Yahweh that I should heed him and let Israel go?" It is clear that the ensuing narrative of the plagues is a sustained, painful process whereby Pharaoh comes to "know Yahweh," that is, to acknowledge Yahweh as sovereign. The narrative portrays the slow, grudging process of acknowledgment:

> So *that you may know* that there is no one like the LORD our God.
> (Ex. 8:10)
> "Pray for me." (Ex. 8:28)
> For this time I will send all my plagues . . . *so that you may know* that there is no one like me in all the earth. (Ex. 9:14)
> "I have sinned. Yahweh is in the right . . . *Pray to Yahweh.*" (Ex. ‘9:27–28)
> "I have sinned *against the LORD your God.*" (Ex. 10:16)
> "Go worship Yahweh as you have said . . . And bring a blessing on me too." (Ex. 12:31–32)

The narrative pays close attention to the ways in which Pharaoh reluctantly, but without misgiving, comes to inhabit the testimonial world of Yahweh. As a consequence, for Pharaoh as for Israel, Yahweh becomes a credible, normal, and indispensable character, without whom the plot makes no sense.[15]

b. The Philistines are presented as knowing about Yahweh from the outset, and acknowledging the awesome power of Yahweh:

> Woe to us! Who can deliver us from these gods who struck the Egyptians with every sort of plague? (1 Sam. 4:8)
> Give glory to the God of Israel. . . . Why should you harden your hearts as the Egyptians and Pharaoh hardened their hearts? After he had made fools of them, did they not let the people go, and they departed? (1 Sam. 6:5–6; cf. Ex. 10:1–2)

c. The Assyrians are the most difficult case among the enemies of Israel. There is no evidence of any yielding of Assyria to the testimonial world of Israel (except see Jonah). In Isaiah 37:22–29, nonetheless, the prophet Isaiah testifies to Yahweh in the face of arrogant Assyrian power:

> By your servants you have mocked Yahweh,
>   and you have said, "With my many chariots

> I have gone up the heights of the mountains,
> > to the far recesses of Lebanon;
> I felled its tallest cedars,
> > its choicest cypresses;
> I came to its remotest height,
> > its densest forest,
> I dug wells and drank waters,
> I dried up with the sole of my foot
> > all the streams of Egypt."
>
> > > > (Isa. 37:24–25)

This statement of Assyrian autonomy is countered by the assertion of Yahweh:

> Have you not heard that I determined it long ago?
> I planned from the days of old what I now bring to pass.
>
> > > > (v. 26)

The rebuke of Assyria is dominated by first-person claims on the part of Yahweh, who is granted both an acting and a speaking part in this rendering of reality.

d. Even Nebuchadnezzar—portrayed in Jeremiah as Yahweh's unwitting servant (25:9; 27:6), and in II Isaiah as recalcitrant to Yahweh and cruel to Israel (cf. 47:6)—in Daniel 4 finally yields to "the Most High":

> I blessed the Most High,
> > and praised and honored the one who lives forever.
> For his sovereignty is an everlasting sovereignty,
> > and his kingdom endures from generation to generation. . . .
> All his works are right,
> > and his ways are just,
> and he is able to bring low
> > those who walk in pride.
>
> > > > (Dan. 4:34, 37)

The exilic community has given nothing away, has conceded or compromised nothing with the hegemony. It gives its own account of reality, which is intensely Yahweh-centered. Nonetheless, it provides examples of the yielding of the hegemonic power to the exilic portrayal of reality. Such a transformation of discourse and perception, and with it a transformation of power relations, however, depends upon the exilic community maintaining its own sense of itself and its own discourse, apart from the dominant narrative of the hegemony.[16]

It is my judgment that the offer of this *testimonial claim* is a modest enterprise. It aims at the marginated community, not more. Its purpose is not to provide a foundation for imperial order or imperial ethics, but to sustain an identity for the community. The utterance of such testimony is on occasion a serendipity that those beyond the horizon of the community of exiles may hear and heed. But the first issue is the enhancement of this testimonial community with its peculiar "more excellent way" in the world. An acknowledgment of this context and an acceptance of an appropriate rhetorical/epistemological stance, I believe, will liberate and empower preaching.

5

Rhetoric and Community

I have suggested that in a decentered, exilic community, no longer included in the cultural hegemony and no longer responsible for that hegemony, an alternative rhetoric is both possible and required. On the one hand, rhetoric concerning the decentered is *testimony*, that is, an advocacy of a very odd truth, a truth that is off-centered and in deep tension with dominant, commonly accepted givens. Such testimony is advocacy, proposed to dispute with and be in conflict with other advocacies. But it is not utterance that is given as a large, universal claim. It is, rather, a local claim made here and now, in these circumstances and with the passions that pertain to this circumstance.

On the other hand, rhetoric among the decentered not only has a different intention, that is, to propose a countertruth that subverts but also *a different style or mode of articulation*. It is not excessively solemn or rationalistic or final or given with too much sobriety. Rather it is an utterance that is playful, open, teasing, inviting, and capable of voicing the kind of unsure tentativeness and ambiguity that exiles must always entertain, if they are to maintain freedom of imagination outside of the hegemony. Such utterances do not yield flat certitudes that can be everywhere counted upon. Rather they yield generative possibilities of something not known or available until this moment of utterance, so that new truth comes as a telling, compelling surprise, birthed precisely in a cunning act of rhetoric that leads the attentive community where it has never been before. It may sometimes lead to a large, vigorous "Amen" or "Hallelujah." But more often it leads to a grunt of recognition or a moan of wistfulness, touching that which has been brooding in the bones and bodies of the exiles, waiting for utterance, but not sure until the new truth-speaker can find voice for the newness.

Thus I have held together for decentered utterance among exiles *the subversive utterance of countertestimony* (i.e., about a God who will not "fit" and about a world governed by this God who will not accommodate or compromise) and *the playful, hyperbolic, ironic utterance* that keeps the uttered future elusively beyond the control of the rulers of this age, who would like to tame the elusiveness into a large, domesticated generalization that can be administered. Thus our topic is *decentered truths* for *decentered people—subversive testimony* in *elusive utterance.*

New Possibilities
for Interpreting Scripture

There has been slowly emerging in scripture study a new practice of interpretation to which preachers for exiles may carefully attend, namely, rhetorical criticism. While this approach may be familiar to some of you, in the context of my general subject, I hope it is useful to present this mode of text interpretation in some coherent fashion. I do not believe that any single method of text interpretation is to be preferred to the exclusion of all others. I believe we must eclectically use all available methods, and that serious interpreters inevitably do. Nonetheless, the intentional embrace of rhetorical criticism seems to me especially important in a situation of a decentered community. I will identify three major contributors to these new possibilities, even though many scholars and practitioners have been engaged in the work.

1. It is commonly recognized in scripture study, and more particularly in Old Testament study, that James Muilenburg is the primary figure in the emergence of rhetorical criticism as an identifiable undertaking. Muilenburg was trained in literary studies before he came to scripture studies, so that he approaches texts with knowing literary and artistic sensitivity. He knew, at the outset of his biblical scholarship, that nothing is accidental in literary articulation, but that artistic intentionality generates always fresh interpretive possibility. In 1968 he presented his discipline-defining lecture titled "Form Criticism and Beyond," in which he proposed rhetorical criticism as a practice of reading texts in ways that paid careful attention to detailed rhetorical matters that marked turns and accents.[1] He understood that it is the detail of the text and the precise cadences of speech that matter to the intention of the text. Thus he paid special attention to the repetition of words and sounds, to conjunctions and prepositions that turned statements in odd ways, to the intentional use of the great freighted words of faith, and to the careful and judicious placement of the divine name in the text.

Muilenburg's work can only be appreciated if it is seen in the context of dominant interpretive methods in his day that were largely preoccupied with historical questions. In that dominant mode of scholarship, it is not an overstatement to say that little attention was paid to the text in its utterance, but meaning was characteristically sought in *what happened behind the text*, in events that could be recovered by historical and archaeological reconstruction. Thus interpreters in a hegemonic community dominated by positivistic certitude could treat texts in summary reductionist fashion. And if the compulsions of history were taken by some to be excessively relativistic, an alternative could be found in creedal interpretation, in which one looked for propositional certitudes that would corral, contain, and illuminate texts. But clearly, both historical and scholastic readings moved quickly beyond the text to larger meanings.[2] Muilenburg, against such reductionism, invited us to read with slowness, patience, and attentiveness, aware that disclosure (= revelation) could arise in artistic articulation and construal. Thus I suggest that the move from historical to rhetorical perspectives of interpretation is a shift congruent with the move from hegemony to exile, though Muilenburg himself had no such sense of a contextual relocation.

2. I suggest a second scholar crucial to new ways of textual interpretation, though he cannot be directly termed a rhetorical critic or even a scripture scholar. Paul Ricoeur, a French philosopher with intense theological concerns of a Reformed kind, occupies a pivotal place in emergent interpretive possibilities.[3] Ricoeur's work is heavily saturated with dense European hermeneutical, literary, and psychoanalytic theory, and his articulations are not noticeably accessible. And certainly Ricoeur's perspective on hermeneutics was not on the horizon of Muilenburg, for Muilenburg worked primarily with the specificity of the text as a literary, artistic datum. Nonetheless, to link Ricoeur's hermeneutical theory to Muilenburg's textual specificity, is, I believe, an enormous gain for us. I mention three programmatic suggestions of Ricoeur, though his work overwhelms us with generative possibilities.

a. Ricoeur is, par excellence, the philosopher of *imagination*.[4] It is he who has shown us that the long-standing, positivistic dismissal of imagination as a fantasy that leads away from reality is a great misfortune for the dominant tradition of epistemology. Imagination, in Ricoeur's practice, is the capacity to work through images, metaphors, and narratives as a way of evoking, generating, and constructing an alternative world that lies beyond and in tension with the taken-for-granted, commonsense world of day-to-day experience. In other words, imagination is the active enterprise of moving beyond one's defining commitments to entertain alternative definitions of self, world, other, and God. This is indeed the dangerous work of all serious artistic effort, that is, to lead the participant beyond what is self-evident to what becomes evident, available, and "real" only in artistic articulation. Ricoeur shows that concrete change—attitude, action, behavior, policy— of any serious, lasting kind arises only through an alternatively imagined world, a world given in artistic articulation that makes old attitudes, actions, behaviors, and policies inappropriate and that in effect summons, authorizes, and legitimates new behavior and policy. Such change is invitational and not at all coercive, for Ricoeur understands that coerced change is no real change at all.

b. Ricoeur has reflected as much as anyone upon the relation between *text and world* and has proposed that all "worlds," that is, all coherent systems of symbolization and meaning, are text suggested, text legitimated, and text propelled.[5] "World" as coherent symbolization is not a given but is an offer of artistic articulation. This way of putting the matter directly resists any "commonsense world of givenness" and insists that even our most readily accepted world is a text-offered world. Thus, for example, the dominant world of competitive consumerism is a text rooted in the positivistic world texted by Francis Bacon and René Descartes.

Ricoeur has distinguished three worlds that are text related. He speaks first of "the world behind the text," the one that is already there as a given before there is any text. This is the world that scripture study has assumed in its "historical" study. This world does not in fact concern us in scripture study, if we are text focused. There is, second, "the world in front of the text," that is, a world of possibility generated by the text, which inspires, empowers, and permits hearers of the text to live and act differently on the basis of the substantive claim of the text. But third and most crucial for Ricoeur, there is "the world in the text," that is, the dramatic transactions that are offered within the confines of the text wherein the several characters of the text—including Yahweh, the God of Israel—interact with each other in ways that "the world behind the text" would never permit. It is the primary work of interpretation, so Ricoeur urges, to live in "the world in the text," in order to see what is permitted and required by the transactions given there.

c. Ricoeur suggests that focus upon "the world in the text," without that world needing to cohere with our taken-for-granted world is an exercise in imagination, which permits the text community to *redescribe, reimagine, and recharacterize* the world in which it lives.[6] The symbolic world we inhabit, unless there is great intentionality, goes by default to the hegemonic definitions of the dominant powers. It is the work of the decentered community, if it is to maintain its distinctive vocation and its subversive identity, to resist the commonly described world, and to engage in, ponder, and enact a redescribed world according to the offer of the text. I may mention in passing the suggestive study of Jacob Neusner, *The Enchantments of Judaism*, which proposes that the daily religious rituals and routines of Jews are done in order that Jews can "imagine their Jewishness," for if there is not such sustained imagination, the community evaporates.[7] I suggest that what Neusner characterizes with specific Jewish reference is a case study of what Ricoeur intends.

I propose that the textual specificity of Muilenburg and the theoretical interpretive categories of Ricoeur together provide a basis for text work with the community of the decentered. Muilenburg without Ricoeur lacks the theoretical categories to see that text reading is an urgent method for community maintenance in a hostile environment. But Ricoeur without Muilenburg remains theoretical, for Ricoeur is not primarily preoccupied with particular text work. Indeed, taken alone, Ricoeur is something of a temptation, for one can consider these theoretical categories, but they by themselves are not modes of practice, and it is the practice of the text that finally makes a difference.

3. Along with Muilenburg and Ricoeur, I mention Phyllis Trible as important to this perspective on texts. Trible is Muilenburg's student and has continued to develop and refine his remarkable insights about the concreteness and artistry of the text. Trible is among the earliest of "feminist" scripture interpreters. It is evident, however, that Trible does not impose upon the text large and heavy ideological requirements, as has indeed happened in some quarters. For all of her feminist commitments, Trible has demonstrated in a series of exquisite studies that it is not ideological heavy-handedness but attention to the text itself that is generative of new interpretation and newly available worlds.[8] It is important to recognize Trible's feminist perspective primarily to notice the way in which she has departed from the positivistic, hegemonic preoccupation with "history." It is indeed a "world within the text" that preoccupies Trible, and she has shown how such texts, when taken with playful seriousness, serve to challenge and deconstruct better-ordered, long-legitimated worlds of domination. Trible's own practice is indeed the practice of a decentered community that patiently finds fresh possibilities for life precisely in the text.

It is worth observing that chronologically, because Trible is a generation later than Muilenburg, her perspective is indeed located as a world decentered from male, positivistic authority in ways that Muilenburg could not have anticipated. I do not suggest that Muilenburg or Trible set out to do something subversive, but that in effect is what has happened through their work. What is subverted by such an approach that does not go behind the text and that does not make any coercive urgings in front of the text, is the old world of certitude. Thus it is a way of doing text that is oddly compatible with a disestablished textual community.

Playful Scriptures

The move to rhetorical criticism, as an access point into the alternative world of the text, takes texts seriously in all of their particularity, without grand historical or grand dogmatic claims. Focus on particular texts insists that what is said in large measure depends precisely on how it is said. The "how" and the "what" cannot be separated, and they together offer the materials for the redescription of the world.[9] Thus it is my urging that in a decentered community, preaching must focus precisely upon the particularity of the texts, without worry about larger reference or coherence. I propose to consider a series of particular texts by way of example of how an exilic community, attentive to texts, can go about a liberated, liberating rereading of the world. In each of these texts, in all of their particularity, I will consider that they *testify to a countertruth* and that, in their testimony, they do so with *playful, invitational openness*, summoning decentered folk to an alternative vision of themselves in the alternative world of Yahweh.

1. *Genesis 27:1–45.* In this long narrative, we are given account of a family in crisis. The crisis is because the father is old, and "his eyes are dim so that he could not see." In such a circumstance, families must think about giving things over to the next generation, to safely entrust what the family most values to the next generation. Hard decisions must be made about who gets what. Members of the family begin to plan, connive, and strategize for advantage. In this family, as in many families, the oldest child is the father's favorite. It is assumed by both of them, father and son, that this son will get the family treasures, the blessing, the power of well-being, that is transmitted by speech and by touch and by hope and by passion.

This rather conventional assumption of father and son, however, is interrupted. There is a second son, a younger twin brother. We may wonder, as second children do, what he will receive if the treasured eldest son receives all. The mother, however, does not just wonder. She acts! She "was listening" when the father spoke to the presumptive heir. She takes daring steps to countermand the intention of the father. She sends the second son on a mission of deception, whereby the second son deceives the old man and receives—irreversibly receives—the blessing not intended for him. The blessing, the life force for well-being that marks this family as peculiar, is given. Under false pretenses! It can only be given once, and it cannot be recalled. And when the father and the older brother discover together that they have been duped and robbed and left powerless and empty-handed, we are invited to observe a scene of bottomless pathos and trembling wretchedness. And the thief, at the behest of his vigilant mother, must now run for his life, a fugitive from his enraged brother who will seek him dead.

On the face of it, without reservation or qualification, this is indeed a dysfunctional family, two sons, each the favorite of a parent who has chosen sides in combat to control the future of the family. That is enough for holding our attention. But there is more. These characters whom I have identified only by role—father, mother, older heir, younger fugitive—these characters have names. Moreover the names are known to us, treasured by us, reused by us. As we hear their names, we have an odd wave of recognition come over us, to discover—in the community that heeds this text—that this is our family. We know the names because they are our relatives, our ancestors, our progenitors—grandparents and cousins and siblings who continue to haunt us. Our family keeps reenacting these same dramas of dysfunction, of deception, of dimness of eyes, and of ending up too many times fugitives, or conversely, of seeking our siblings dead.

Because this is our family, moreover, we are permitted to enter more closely into the intimacy of the narrative. Or perhaps not permitted. Perhaps we shamelessly push our way into the narrative. We do so not out of curiosity, but because we must know. We must know what happened that day, who said what to whom and in what tone. We must know because it is unmistakably clear that what was said that day lingers like a power and like a trouble even until now, we being the same family of unrelieved vexation.

So we must hear it again. We watch, now knowing the names of our kinfolk. We watch as Esau comes back into the tent:

ESAU: Let my father arise, and eat of his son's game, that you may bless me (Gen. 27:31).

ISAAC: Who are you?

ESAU: I am your son, your first born, Esau (v. 32).

NARRATOR: Isaac trembled violently . . . "I have blessed him . . . yes, and he shall be blessed!" (v. 33) When Esau heard the words of his father, he cried out with an exceedingly great and bitter cry and said to his father, "Bless me, even me, O my father (v. 34) . . . Have you not reserved a blessing for me?" (v. 36). "Have you but one blessing, my father? Bless me, even me also, O my father." And Esau lifted up his voice and wept (v. 38).

We are drawn to this moment of pathos, and we are held there. We know that in the back of the tent the cunning mother is packing a lunch for her fleeing pet. But we will not look away from Esau, even to scold Rebekah or to scorn Jacob. We have the sense that in this moment of terrible intimacy, we are watching an event of cosmic proportion, of ominous grief and rage that will echo in Palestine and in our families and in the family of nations until the end of time. And we sob with Esau. Is that all? Is there no more? Nothing left of the generosity of God? We are, moreover, given an unwelcome moment of self-recognition because we have played all these parts. We drive the drama to even more intense risk in our own day, our own dramas, our own miseries, our own cunning, our own loss, our own grief. We with father Isaac tremble violently, and with brother Esau we weep an exceedingly great and bitter weeping. With the narrative, we require "limit adverbs" now for what we notice about these ancients and about ourselves.[10]

This is indeed our story. That is why we attend to it. But it is not our story simply because it is the story of everyone—though it is in a way that. It is our story because we have been prompted by it, had it take over our imagination, been occupied by it, and been caused to linger over it. That is what we mean, in our mumbling way, by "the authority of scripture." It is our story; it requires us to notice a member of this cast of characters who is almost not mentioned, but who lingers in power at the edge of the text, and at the edge of utterance. We practiced readers are able to spot Yahweh, the God of Abraham and Sarah, even where God remains unuttered. In this particular narrative, God is hidden, present in the term "blessing," a term that preoccupied both parents and both brothers. The notion of blessing can be nothing more than familiar gestures of good intention. In this narrative and in this family, however, blessing is never only that, since Genesis 12, since Yahweh, the God of blessing, said to Abraham:

> I will bless you and make your name great,
> so that you will be a blessing. (Gen. 12:2)

We have known that blessing as the long-term, sovereign resolve of Yahweh to bring good into the world. And now, in Isaac's mistaken utterance and erroneous deployment of power, the same God with the same long-term sovereign resolve to bring good into the world operates:

> May God give you of the dew of heaven . . .
> blessed be everyone who blesses you.
> (Gen. 27:28–29)

Yahweh is at work in this narrative. Jacob not only gets what belongs to his brother. Jacob receives what Yahweh has to give, a blessing. Jacob, stealthy younger brother, saturated with deception, is a carrier of God's goodness and will for life. There is a strange abrasion that dominates the story, a fugitive younger son and the sovereign ruler of heaven and earth, the fugitive carrying the freight of the sovereign. Or another way, a dysfunctional family as vehicle for the truth of the gospel, the link made through lying and weeping, through violent trembling. What comes clear to Isaac and Esau in that ugly moment is that God's purposes had outrun them, and they could not have the future as they had intended it. The story of this misguided, dysfunctional family goes on into many generations, until our time, nothing denied about dysfunction, but along the way, the verdict is more than once uttered from the lips of Isaac's grandson: "You meant it for evil, but God meant it for good" (Gen. 50:20). And we are left to ponder.

2. *2 Kings 6:8–23*.[11] In a very different genre, there is another quite

particular text we treasure. It is among the Elijah-Elisha text, all odd and defiant of our controlling reason. In this particular episode, the narrator begins, "Once . . ." (v. 8). Once, it could have been any time, when the king of Syria was warring against Israel. It could have been any king, because the hostility and the threat are very old, and continue to operate, because the disputed "Golan Heights" is very real, real estate.

The problem is that the king of Syria has a security leak. Every military plan and ploy he devises is known immediately in Israel. Except, we are told . . . except the king of Syria is told, the problem is not a security leak. The problem is more acute: It is "Elisha, the prophet who is in Israel" (v. 12). We do not know how he knows, and no explanation is offered. It is accepted by all parties—including the narrator—that Elisha is larger than life. And so he must be stopped, if Syria's military program is to have a chance. He is like the ominous spy who makes the normal conduct of war impossible.

We next watch a ludicrous scene. The Syrian king dispatches an entire army to surround the home of the prophet. The army arrives in great numbers, many horses, much noise, and shouting, and confusion, and intimidation (v. 15). The contrast is stunning. The great army of Syria and the lone magic man, larger than life, sitting defenseless in his home. He is alone, except for his servant boy who is completely devoted to him. The prophet is unflappable . . . what do armies mean to him? But his servant boy is different. He still operates with conventional calculus. He looks out the window to see about all the noise, and he is terrified. He sees immediately that all is lost. "Alas, my master, what shall we do?" (v. 15). His master, the unflappable man of God, assures him: "Fear not, for those with us are more than those with them" (v. 16).

The boy begins to count. He counts a myriad on the Syrian side. He counts his own side, "One . . . two." That is all. He wonders about prophetic arithmetic, and he is still frightened. But then in an abrupt shift of mood, Elisha prays. We have this account of an enormous military threat, a shift of categories, and then a prayer: "O LORD, I pray thee, open his eyes that he may see" (v. 17).

Elisha names the name: "O Yahweh!" Elisha makes present in this moment all the promises and powers of "The Equalizer," the one known in the life of Israel and alive on the lips of Israel. It is "O Yahweh" that authorizes his earlier, "Fear not." The narrative shows the world of Israel to be peopled with a power Syria had not acknowledged or reckoned with. The prayer is ominous for Syria:

> Yahweh opened the eyes of the young man and he saw. And behold, the mountain was full of horses and chariots of fire round about Elisha. (2 Kings 6:17)

The summons of Yahweh, the petition, and the gift of sight resituate the boy, reconstitute reality, redress the balance of power and terror. The blind see!

> The man of God prays a second time to the LORD:
> "Strike this people, I pray thee, with blindness." (2 Kings 6:18)

Promptly the Syrians become blind and helpless, completely vulnerable to the leadership of Elisha. The powerful ones are made impotent by the redefining capacity of Yahweh. In two quick petitions the world has been transformed. The first have become last, and the last first!

Then follows a narrative in which Elisha leads the helpless Syrians captive into the capital city of Samaria. They are helpless. And so the king of Israel, who enters the story belatedly, wants to kill his enemy now that they are in his power (v. 21). Except the prophet will not let the king take over the narrative. Instead of yielding to the deathly wish of the king, the prophet prays yet a third time, this time to restore sight to the blind enemy. And then the prophet commands a great feast and the erstwhile enemies eat together (v. 22).

The prophet has prayed three times and has caused everyone to see differently. The narrator ends with the laconic affirmation, "The Syrians came no more on raids into the land of Israel" (v. 23). The narrative begins in hostility and ends in at least provisional reconciliation. The prophet has broken, for a time, the vicious cycle of fear and abuse.

This narrative stands at some distance from us, because most of us care not too much about Golan and none of us cares about the ancient Syrians. It takes some doing to draw closer to the story. But it is our story. It is ours, humanly speaking, because we find ourselves often cast as the servant boy, on the right side but frightened, outnumbered, without resources, aware of the jeopardy, wishing for safety, occasionally given fresh vision to see differently. But the story is not ours only because of this common human reality.

It is ours because the cadences of speech here are our particular cadences in the community of the baptized.[12] We know about such desperate petition made with such long odds, because we are nurtured in prayer that always hopes and yearns for this awesome Third Party to be present in our contexts of fearfulness. Thus when Elisha prays, "O LORD, I pray thee," we pray along, knowing the cadences, and echoing the petition. We know about praying for support in the presence of long odds and sometimes receiving it. And we know the cadences when he prays over the Syrians, "O LORD, open the eyes of these men, that they may see." The prayer is a follow-up to an act of daring reconciliation that gives dignity and freedom to those who have been enemies. We know, if not about such prayers, about the yearning to be able to pray such prayers and to trust in what we receive.

Thus we watch while Yahweh completely reorganizes reality at the behest of this man saturated with faith. It does not occur to us, as insiders to this narrative, to ask how this could happen, nor to ask if it did really happen. It is a narrative of our own cadences, and we enter into it with a kind of elemental recognition. It is like hearing one's mother tongue in a faraway, foreign-language society. We recognize kinship and are glad for it. And because the cadences are familiar to us, we entertain the substantive claims of the narrative. We know about heavenly power carried by earthly characters. We know about prayers and gestures that give sight to the blind, that heal the lepers, that cause the lame to walk and the dead to dance. For an instant, we live in the world of impossible possibility, a world of inexplicable inversions, incomprehensible transformations, and inscrutable miracles, credible because it is sounded in our mother tongue. We are reminded, moreover, not to accept the world as it is defined by the Syrian armies or other ominous hegemonic powers.

As the story ends, the narrator departs, the scroll is put back in its safe place, and the book is closed. We utter the formula, "The word of the Lord . . . thanks be to God." And we hear shadowed from the feast in Samaria:

> If your enemy is hungry, feed him; if he is thirsty, give him drink;
> for by so doing you will heap burning coals upon his head. Do not
> be overcome by evil, but overcome evil with good. (Rom.
> 12:20–21)[13]

Later on, when we can no longer recall the story line, perhaps all that will be left is the prophet's word to the fearful boy, "fear not, fear not, fear not." Heeding that is already to see differently.

3. *Isaiah 45:1–6, 10–11.* These verses are an eruption of poetry made to Jews in exile, surely at the brink of despair and hopelessness. There surely are among the Jews calculation and perhaps effort put into the political possibility of emancipation from Babylonian deportation. The poet however stands remote from any Jewish strategies and blurts out an unthought, unthinkable, scandalous alternative possibility: "Thus says Yahweh to his messiah, to Cyrus" (v. 1). Or more scandalously in the Greek, "to his Christ, to Cyrus." The poet joins the intimately Jewish term "messiah," the cipher for all royal, Davidic hope, the image for chosen Jewish agents who effect Yahweh's transformations in the historical process, to the foreign name Cyrus, rising *goi* (Gentile) from Iran who was not even yet on the screen of Jewish expectation. Yahweh is instigator of this Gentile in this oddly Jewish enterprise of letting Jewish exiles return home to Jewish land. A *goi* will enact the most fervent of Jewish hopes!

That explosive rhetoric at the beginning of the oracle permits Yahweh to wax eloquent about Yahweh's own magisterial resolve:

> I will go before you . . .
> I will hack in pieces doors of bronze . . .
> I will give you treasures of darkness.
>
> (Isa. 45:2–3)

It is all "so that you may know":

> It is I, Yahweh, the God of Israel . . .
> I am, there is no other;
>   besides me there is no God.
>
> (vv. 3–5)

That is a mouthful of Yahwism in the mouth of Yahweh. I imagine, however, that these Jewish exiles heard little of the assertion of Yahweh. They
were still back, stunned in the first syllables of the utterance,
"messiah/Cyrus." Here is Yahweh doing Yahweh's most characteristic, familiar thing—saving—but in a radically unfamiliar, uncharacteristic
mode.

The assertion is not only of Yahweh's sovereign purpose but also of
Israel's special status as the beloved of Yahweh. The one who speaks is "the
God of Israel." This God purposes to liberate Jews. Yahweh acts,

> for the sake of my servant Jacob,
>   and Israel my chosen.
>
> (v. 4)

All of this is familiar, all reaffirmed, Jerusalem celebrated. But likely the Jews
addressed in exile never heard this wondrous affirmation, for they were still
back on the first utterance, stunned at the scandal, Messiah/Cyrus!

Here is a marvelous claim for Yahweh, a marvelous assurance of Israel,
but all accomplished by Cyrus, the *goi* messiah, Jewish royal oil poured on
a *goi*-anointed head. We do not know what the Jews in exile said in
response to this announcement. There is a pause in the text, and then the
poet has Yahweh speak again. We imagine Israel's resistant response on the
basis of Yahweh's next comment. Presumably Israel said, "Oh no. Not by
a *goi*! We will not go home that way. If that is the only offer, we will stay
deported, better dead than red." Perhaps they said that. We do know for
sure what Yahweh said next to the exiles:

> Woe to anyone who says to a father, "What are you begetting?"
>   or to a woman, "With what are you in labor?" . . .
> Will you question me about my children,
>   or command me concerning the work of my hands?
>
> (vv. 10–11)

How dare you question me! You forget your proper place. You distrust our
relation. You doubt my intention. You have no right to question, no

grounds for doubt, no excuse for resistance. You will take it the way I give it, even if it is not your way, because "my ways are not your ways." Yahweh will order Jewish life as Yahweh chooses. If it offends Jews in their propriety and self-assurance and orthodoxy, too bad! Home is a path opened by a Gentile . . . and you will go!

The text is an offer and a rebuke to God's chosen Jews. The baptized belatedly hear the text, and it is so remote. For we are not in exile, and yet we have an exile-specific text. The text witnesses to Cyrus, and we care nothing at all for ancient kings and empires. Indeed, we do not even touch the reference to exile, leave alone the Persians. The text is particular and therefore remote.

However, we have considered that our own cultural displacement and alienation are not unlike exile. Cyrus is no longer person or agent but now is metaphor. Now "Cyrus" has become whatever historical agent or means by which we can identify or imagine who is doing God's liberating work among us, but who is doing so in ways that upset and with credentials that offend. In our distanced hearing of this Cyrus assertion, we are unable to host Cyrus in our imagination until we have paid close attention, hostile attention, to Nebuchadnezzar, for Cyrus is an antidote to Nebuchadnezzar. Nebuchadnezzar, here implied but never named, is the harsh Babylonian master who deported Jews from their homeland, who disrupted Jewish identity, and who imposed pressures of alienation upon faith. As we are with Cyrus, so we have no business to conduct with Nebuchadnezzar, not unless Nebuchadnezzar, like Cyrus, becomes a lively metaphor referring to all those forces, pressures, and agents who impose displacement and alienation upon us and put us in hostile places. With this text we are not summoned to the sixth century B.C.E. We are rather required to recharacterize and redescribe our own situation in terms of Nebuchadnezzar and Cyrus. But that is not very difficult. We all know of the impositions of hostility and bondage and the loss of freedom in our life. As baptized folk, we expect and insist upon Yahweh's liberative action. We insist that God will in powerful and visible ways rescue us from the non-life in which we are caught.

So we ponder the bondage that is no stranger to us. We name the marvelous name of Yahweh, to whom we belong in trust and confidence, and we count heavily upon our status as God's beloved. This all sounds okay, and we take this cast of characters and run it toward Jesus. When we arrive at the poor man of Nazareth, however, for all our comfortable cultural clichés about Jesus, we notice how strange he is—poor, affrontive, subversive, elusive. We notice how that early community of faith nearly choked getting the noble title *messiah* together with this *crucified Jesus*, choking almost as much as on the Cyrus offer. We ponder how cozy and comfortable we have gotten with Jesus, and now are reminded how odd and incompatible he is.

More than that, however. The text runs to Jesus and so we read. It runs beyond Jesus to other figures we would ill name messiah, odd players in

the anointed work of Yahweh, agents so unlike us, so unlike David, so affrontive. You know, abrasive blacks and aggressive women, and those
whose vision require us to redefine what we think about our cozy definitions of power and money and sexuality and humanness. It takes no great
imagination to think that we might resist such emancipation, might prefer to stay bondaged in fear and isolation, if that is the only alternative
offered by God. If this is God's doing (surely not!), we might refuse. We
might be the little fetus questioning the groaning mother in labor. And
then the impatient rebuke against us: "Will you question me?" And we
are pressed to take God's offer of newness the way it comes, even if his
way is not our way. We never thought ourselves to be among the re-
sisters, but the juxtaposition of messiah/Christ is more than too much.
And we are left to wish for a liberation of God a bit more accommodat-
ing. But the text offers none of that.

4. *2 Samuel 12:24–25.* This text on the birth of Solomon seems distant
from us. But it is okay, because it deals with the birth of a baby:

> Then David consoled his wife Bathsheba, and went to her, and lay
> with her; and she bore a son, and he named him Solomon. The
> LORD loved him.

It is as though the narrative recovers its equilibrium after the Bathsheba-
Uriah sordidness of David. Now we are back to the main story line.
Solomon is a good one, soon to be a great king, manager of an economy of
peace and prosperity, dispenser of wisdom that cuts to the heart of human
reality, and above all, builder of the temple, a pious man who makes
Yahweh's abiding presence in Israel visible and reliable. Solomon is the
success story of Israel's faith. His establishment is enough to show that
Yahwism works. He is the model of the megachurch, for Jerusalem is a
megachurch, enough established and enough inscrutable to justify the
Masons. And even for non-Masons, he is a mesmerizing success story.

This wondrous text of birth, which leads to civil war among the sons of
David and the brothers of Solomon, knows that Solomon, like the rest of
us, never travels alone. He comes with his family. He is always in a group
picture, as are we all. More specifically, he comes with his mamma. He is
the son of Bathsheba: "David consoled his wife Bathsheba, and she bore
him a son and he named him Solomon." We know, in general, that mothers of princes were in that ancient world powerful palace players. And we
know, specifically, that Bathsheba was a cunning, accomplished part of the
manipulative theater that brought Solomon to the throne, in a cruel
contest with his siblings. This king, like every power player, is no solo
achievement. He is there with his mother. He cannot be separated from her.

Nor can he be separated from his father David, a blessed, attractive man,
but one who could not manage, short of rapacious activity that had to do

with land and women and truth. Solomon comes from a line of exploiters, and he continues the family business!

You know how his mother and father got together in the preceding chapter. David stayed home from the office. In chapter 11, the narrative is terse. David, who is at the top of his royal game, can have whatever he wants. And what he wants is Solomon's mother-to-be. And then in quick order, "He saw . . . he sent to inquire . . . he sent to get . . . he lay with her . . . she sent word, 'I'm pregnant'" (2 Sam. 11:2–5). I do not know how long it took. Minimum of twelve minutes. Likely more, but not too much, because David is a busy man. Just a moment of passion and lust and freedom, a moment never to be undone, irreversible. About as long as Senator Kennedy's moment at Chappaquiddick. Our past is so insistent, forever, never to be undone. There was a subsequent innocence: "She bore a son, and he named him Solomon. The LORD loved him." This text remembers forever. And we are children of this text, unable to forget.

Later on, in speaking of subsequent kings and the threat of the north, the narrative observes of Abijam, Solomon's inconsequential grandson:

> His heart was not true to the LORD his God like the heart of his father David. Nevertheless for David's sake, the LORD his God gave him a lamp in Jerusalem . . . because David did what was right in the eyes of the LORD, and did not turn aside for anything that he commanded him all the days of his life, *except* in the matter of Uriah the Hittite. (1 Kings 15:3–5)

Except—*except* for twelve irreversible minutes of autonomy! This is not a sex-sin and we are not prudes. This was a moment of autonomy, a moment of grunting and sweating in self-satisfaction, an occasion when autonomous sperm was transferred to an egg, perhaps done gently, probably roughly. Except, and this family, our family, is haunted by it forever.

A brief hidden moment, hidden except for this too-shrewd historian, hidden and underground midst the temple and the opulence, and the power, and the well-being, of this prince named *Shalom*, who lives in the city named Jeru-*shalom*, all peace—except for twelve minutes.

The memory lingers underground in Israel, known only to the family that relishes the comfort and mostly denies the sordid beginning, known and available so late, so late as Matthew, who must construct a family tree for Jesus. You know how he does it, having named the harlot Rahab and the whore Tamar, mothers in Israel, and then to the great kings: "And David was the father of Solomon by the wife of Uriah" (Matt. 1:6). In the birth account of 2 Samuel 12, it is at least "David consoled his wife Bathsheba." By Matthew, however, she has lost that identity, for her final status is "wife of Uriah," the one who is murdered and murdered forever.

We can manage that genealogical note, however, because Matthew manages, by the end of the family tree to assure us that Jesus, of the Virgin, is not of that sordid line anyway (Matt. 1:16). With a pure mother, we may at last depart this despicable birth that looms quiet in Israel. Solomon now at last can have his own portrait, without his mother, because Jesus has another family.

What a relief to have Solomon without the whole family. Except that the next mention of this great king in the Gospel of Matthew is put this way by his putative heir:

> Why do you worry about clothes. . . . Yet I tell you, even Solomon in all his glory was not clothed like one of these. . . . Seek God's righteousness. . . . (Matt. 6:28–33)

That is a long way from the temple and all its surrounding splendor. Jesus cites Solomon as the quintessence of opulent success and security, and reminds his listening disciples that there is an alternative to Solomon that is filled both with more cost and more joy.

It is, of course, obvious that all of these textual explorations concerning Bathsheba, David, and Solomon in the New Testament are not immediately present in the birth announcement of 2 Samuel 12:24–25. This community of exiles, however, knows that no person is an isolated, autonomous agent, for exiles must always

> Look to the rock from which you were hewn,
>   and to the quarry from which you were dug.
> Look to Abraham your father
>   and to Sarah who bore you.
>   (Isa. 51:1–2)

In the same way, this community knows that every text travels in a company of linked texts, each of which is heard along with all the others. In this case, this is the announcement of the birth of this greatly beloved child who is destined for wondrous things, named *Shalom*. But like all beloved children, he comes with his family. He comes along with his father who did what was right in the eyes of Yahweh, *except* for one thing. He comes along with a mother who is still, inexorably and forever, "wife of Uriah the Hittite." Perhaps with such a father and such a mother he would strive to be well and wise and safe and powerful. He became so from this wondrous birth, enough so that this "greater son of David" imagined that "Solomon in all his glory" is not as well off as birds and lilies.

We who listen later are remote from this new, princely baby. But we are not so remote that we do not enter into the innocence, wonder, and blessedness of this beloved son. Nor are we so remote that we do not recognize his father as our kinsman David and his mother as our kinswoman Bathsheba. And we notice how our best innocence is overlaid in the characteristic complicity of our family, so burdened, so encumbered that unburdened birds and unencumbered lilies of the field strike us as an alternative. We know ourselves necessarily marked and compromised, and yet with a yearning to see God's righteousness and so to be beyond some of our anxiety. We are so distanced from this baby, but so deeply entwined, beloved and burdened, endorsed and encumbered, with a yearning even beyond this family of ours.

Particularity and Density

It has struck me, as I worked these texts and listened to them, that they are profoundly particular:

> An exchange one day between an old man and his unwittingly denied son, in the shattering, pathos-filled moment of their shared self-recognition.
> A prayer for sight uttered twice, only twice, for a boy and for an alien army, with a conflict ended in a feast.
> An oracle of hope formed by the strange, offensive juxtaposition of anointed and *goi*.
> A birth announcement of a beloved son set deep in a family of failure.

All are one-time uttered events, situated long ago in particularities that preclude typification or replication, so poignantly particular. And yet, we propose to gather round such particularities, this displaced community of exiles, so needful and so expectant. It is nearly a scandal that we seek to connect in a crucial way these particular texts and this displaced community. It is indeed a wonder that the displaced come here, to these texts, precisely to such old, located texts, ready to be addressed by them again, afresh, anew, with a word of life. We ponder how particularity hooks up with displacement.

I suggest that the clue to exiles coming to particular texts is the *density of the transaction*, a density that need not be always recognized, but that must be attended to, even if intuitively.

1. I take the notion of density from the anthropological concept of "thick description." Gilbert Ryle used the term to refer to speech and gesture that impart a particular message to someone in particular in a socially established code known only to insiders of the community.[14] The concept was made maximally important and available by Clifford Geertz in his essay, "Thick Description: Toward an Interpretive Theory of Cultures," in which he stressed the power and significance of webs of social gesture that constitute symbolic action.[15] More recently Michael Walzer, in *Thick and Thin*, has observed how ethical maximalism concerns ethical discourse

that is "richly referential, culturally resonant, locked into a locally established symbolic system or network of meanings."[16]

All of these articulations—from Ryle, Geertz, and Walzer—accent the particularity of sign, symbol, and gesture known only to insiders who receive their identity and their chance in the world from such coded gestures, coded so that they appear to outsiders to be at least empty if not nonsensical. This notion of density (= thickness) coheres well with my thesis about exiles. Hegemonic community tends to trade in thin or minimalist discourse, and that is adequate where consensus meanings are assured and not under assault. It is precisely among the nonhegemonic, that is, the marginated, the exiles, that thick, coded discourse is crucial to the maintenance and sustenance of an alternative identity.

I submit, then, that preaching a biblical text among baptized exiles is precisely *a practice of density* that is essential to the maintenance of identity and crucial for missional freedom and vocational energy midst an indifferent or hostile hegemony. Thus I will consider in turn reference to three dimensions of this density:

    a.   What kind of text is proclaimed?
    b.   What kind of people gather for proclamation?
    c.   Who is the God that is the subject of such textual, proclamatory discourse?

2. The text, as I have tried to show in my examples of particularity, is enormously dense. It signals and references in a myriad of complex directions. Currently that density is referred to as intertextuality.[17] The text is situated among many other tests, also known in the gathered community, and it makes all kinds of direct, explicit, and subtle allusions to these texts, some of which may be voiced and some of which are only hauntingly at the edge of awareness.[18] It is abundantly clear that in a practiced liturgical community, many of these signals and allusions are known and felt and recognized and embraced, so that any single utterance mediates a large, rich world. Thus, as I have shown, the birth announcement of Solomon alludes not only to the greatness to come, but also to the sordidness that is intractable, to the belovedness not defeated by sordidness, and to the one greater than Solomon and greater than his father David. Those who hear the birth announcement are invited to make connections that re-web our identity in this family.

We have, to be sure, been practitioners of a thinning of the text, so that the text is read only at surface. On the one hand, thinning of the thick text and consequent loss of density has happened through theological reductionism, in which rich texts are flattened to serve creedal certitude. On the other hand, there is no doubt that historical criticism is a thinning maneuver, designed to make irascibly complex texts amenable to Enlightenment rationality, to eliminate the haunting inscrutability of the text.

In the face of theological reductionism and critical thinning, however, texts have persisted in their density, refused to be diluted, ever again available in richness, knowing that if denseness is uttered, "They will come."

3. The kind of people who come to hear the dense texts proclaimed are characteristically dense people (by which I do not mean stupid!). Of course people come to church for all kinds of reasons, some ignoble, but surely with all kinds of mixed motives. Over all, however, people come to church knowing that they here enter a different discourse, in which we talk oddly about odd matters. Some, to be sure, want surface certitude and some hope for simple moralism. But everybody here finally demands more than surface certitude and simple moralism, which, of course, is why textual preaching is potentially the most satisfying. It is because there is resonance between dense text and dense life, more dense than is satisfied by a thin experientialism.[19]

The folk who come to worship live dense lives. The term "density," as concerns human persons, suggests to me the phrase "depth psychology," which might be rendered as a "psychology of density." Humans, if not narcotized by the hegemony, live with multidimensioned memory, with layers of recall, some buoyant, some unresolved. When we come to church we are not only able, managing, achieving daytime operators. We are at the same time haunted, bewildered, frightened creatures of the night, ready for new configurations of reality and meaning, ready to be "re-webbed" in more risky ways, ready even in our resistance. It takes an exceedingly dense text to meet such exceedingly dense humanity.

More than this, however. Those present for preaching are not simply densely human, though that is no small thing. We are either those already marked by baptism, or those who are candidates for baptism, within or at the brink of second birth, second marking, born from above. Our density is not simply because we are *Homo sapiens*, but because we are baptized, committed, beloved, commanded persons with all the complexities that accompany passionate commitment and unconditional grace. We come in our unresolve. But we come. That means we have a certain staying power for this odd identity. We show up. And we listen. We expect to be addressed, partly because of obligation, but partly because we live in an "abiding astonishment."[20] The familiar words of prayer, creed, and song roll over our lips, bespeaking realities that defy our thinness.

We did not dream up or invent the code in which we participate. We have come to it late as recipients, joining those already there before us. That is, we are intergenerational, following those who are committed before us, going ahead of grandchildren on whose behalf we trust. We know about Abraham our rock, and about Sarah our quarry, and about Lois and Eunice. We know that

> all of these died in faith without having received the promises, but from a distance they saw and greeted them . . . that they would not, apart from us, be made perfect. (Heb. 11:13, 40)

Those who struggle for and in and with baptism refuse thinness in their lives. We refuse the thinness of self-indulgence and self-sufficiency. We refuse the thin identity of consumer given us so insistently by market ideology. We refuse to be consumers, or to be consumed by conformity or by isolated individualism. And so we attend to symbolic discourse, which mediates to us obligation, ragged ministry, the artistry of Bach, the flow of little children, the requirement of neighbor love. We have not and will not quit into the all-absorbant hegemony. And so we rally to this text.

4. The text is a witness. It witnesses to the Primal Character in the script of our life, the One who stands at the center of our narrative of liberation and healing, the One who stands before the first verbs of the creed with heaven and earth to follow, the One showing up fleshed in Jesus of Nazareth. Text is indispensable, for this Character inhabits the text. But we know well that the text points beyond itself, testifying to the One who lives there.

This character, as Jack Miles has shown so well, is endlessly quixotic and enigmatic, filled with contradictions, *always present*, but distressingly absent at the dangerous times; *all knowing*, but sometimes wondering, questioning, testing, unsure; *all powerful*, but clearly not master of the evil that is still loose among us.[21] Our people have known forever that it takes many texts in tension with each other to offer this God, because less than many texts yields a boring idol, safe but not this live God among us.

We know about the thinning of God, the attempt to flatten and refine Yahweh's dense interior. Creedal reductionism does not want to acknowledge this God who leaks out beyond good doctrine. However, the maddening leakage is there in the text, waiting to be spoken of in faith and in dismay. Critical reductionism cuts the nerve of faith by slicing tensions into different sources, documents, and trajectories, with none of it left for elusive, holy reality. But thinness is no adequate habitat for the Holy One of Israel. So the tales must be told—of grace and rage, of presence and absence, of honor and shame, of forgetting and remembering, of noticing and ignoring—tales of our lived life, tales in which God is endlessly embedded, wild and beyond domestication, to the thousandth generation.

The sermon is that convergence of *dense text*, *dense people*, and *dense God*. The preacher is the one who reconvenes the web of significance, enacts yet again the coded winks that revivify the church.[22]

The congregation comes with human readiness and with baptismal readiness, prepared to be voiced to the freedom and courage and grace that belong to our identity. Ready, except for the fearfulness that dwells in our humanness; ready, except for the doubt that occupies space in our baptism. We are ready, because we know all about

A feeble father and a rejected son who together weep and tremble fiercely.

A prayer that gives sight to the young and innocent, to see a
world peopled with allies when we thought the enemies outnumbered us in chariots and in horses.

A *goi* governor who carried the Jewish label "messiah," as we
watch the rise and fall of power bold but flimsy.

A beloved baby born in sordidness, loved to *shalom*, surpassed
beyond anxiety.

We know because our lives match the text in density.

But of course we know so little, having listened so poorly and hosted so
carelessly. We are not ready to hear, but the text itself readies us. The text
not only gives us substantive truth; it also asserts among us the odd
categories through which truth must be received. We come in human,
baptismal readiness, and the text overpowers us on occasion in our
unacknowledged, resident unreadiness.

The preacher speaks in such ancient particularity. Often something
happens—not always—and there is an unavoidable connection between
ancient particularity and contemporary density. And in that dense,
inscrutable transaction, exiles are emboldened, healed, liberated, restored,
transformed, and raised to new life, in the face of hegemony, unintimi-
dated, unafraid, unyielding, insistent through the massive layers of intentionality, newly birthed in this moment of utterance. To an outsider, it all
seems so thin and odd. To the coded insider, however, it is a moment out
on the edge of new life, refusing the ponderous, incessant threats of death.

6

Overhearing
the Good News

I have urged the point that preaching in the U.S. church, in a cultural condition of post-Christendom, is analogous to preaching to exiles. More broadly, biblical preaching is addressed to the particular community of believers committed through baptism to the claims of biblical faith. Christian preaching is addressed to the community of the baptized in order to articulate, sustain, and empower a distinctive identity in the world. Mutatis mutandis, Jewish proclamation of these texts is addressed to Jewish congregations in order to maintain a distinctive Jewish theological identity in the world.[1]

"Preaching to exiles" suggests that the believing, listening community addressed in Christian preaching lives in a demanding circumstance, beset by a culture that is hostile or indifferent to its faith, but a community in any case that refuses to credit its faith claims, that is, refuses to imagine the world according to a narrative that has Yahweh as its key character. The analogue of "exile" requires the cognate analogy that the dominant culture in which believers live and believe is roughly "Babylonian," that is, a culture that exercises socioeconomic hegemony and with it a set of myths (ideology) that serves as legitimatization and amounts to a dominating, totalizing theological claim. As Charles Reich can speak of "the money government," so we may speak in parallel fashion of the "money ideology."[2] The analogy of exile and Babylon, in my judgment, currently pertains to the dominant free market ideology that seems to carry all before it, and in the face of which any alternative construal of reality with Yahweh as the central character is demanding work indeed.[3] I have no doubt that this is the true situation of most Christian preaching in our particular U.S. social context.

Inside and Outside

More, however, needs to be said than simply to situate the church in exile. I shall seek to voice something of that "more" in this chapter. The truth is that biblical preaching—from Paul in Acts 17 to modern street preaching to contemporary church preaching that has as a listening community many skeptics and "cultured despisers of religion"—has never confined itself to its own believing community. It has characteristically reached beyond that community in order to issue a summons and invitation to those who live outside the community and who, either intentionally or accidentally, subscribe to the claims of the Babylonian hegemony. Biblical preaching has proceeded on the assumption that the truth of biblical faith pertains to such "outsiders" even as much as "insiders," because the God who stands at the center of the church's narrative imagination is not primarily the lord of the church but the creator and governor of heaven and earth.

The issue of insider-outsider, for Christian preaching, is currently framed in several ways.[4] It has become almost conventional to conclude that the postliberalism of George Lindbeck, Stanley Hauerwas, and William H. Willimon deals with the *inside* of the church to the neglect of the *outside*, whereas David Tracy is so concerned for credibility *outside* the church that the *interiority* of church faith is neglected. It is likely that in the end such judgments are, in both cases, caricatures.

As the polemics of contemporary theology proceed, it is as though these positions, commonly associated with Tracy at the University of Chicago and Lindbeck at Yale, represent the only alternatives.[5] Moreover, except for a few devotees, I imagine that no one who engages in serious practice is fully at ease with either such position, and in fact does not in any case operate with a pure model of interpretation. It is almost inescapable, I suppose, that the sensitivities of a scripture teacher would be much more congenial to the so-called Yale School. I do not, however, for a moment imagine that the church (and its preachers) can speak only to the church. Thus any "sectarian withdrawal" from speech "in the public square" is to be rejected out of hand.

William Placher is, to be sure, more sympathetic to the "Yale School," but increasingly positions himself in something of a mediating position.[6] In his book *Narratives of a Vulnerable God*, without conceding much to "public theology," Placher allows that Tracy's two other publics—the academy and society—do indeed "overhear" the theological claims made in the church by the church and for the church.[7] I take his phrase "overhear" to mean that the church itself is the primary addressee in this discourse, so that the canons of credibility operative in the church are the decisive ones. That is, what is to be said must be tested first of all by the core memory of the church.

It is important at the same time, however, to insist that such "overhearing" is not happenstance or accidental or incidental. Rather the church, at its most courageous and its most faithful, deliberately and intentionally makes its claims for the sake of the nonchurch public.

It is not to be thought that "church talk" is casually overheard by the larger public, as though a casual "drive by" the church would make a difference. Rather, out of its own baptismal conversation, the churches of the gospel celebrated in the baptismal community are echoed in larger context in ways germane to public questions, public issues, and public possibilities. The crucial issue of course is the phrase "in ways germane" that leaves much open that cannot be determined ahead of time.

To put it in my categories stated above, preaching *addresses exiles* but believes at the same time that its claims addressed to exiles have *pertinence and compelling authority to the Babylonians* as well. It is important that members of the hegemony are a second and not a first addressee, a role reserved for the exilic community. But members of the hegemony nevertheless are addressees, which causes preaching to be continually engaged with authority claims outside the privileged community of the first addressees. It may be helpful, following Douglas John Hall, to suggest that the church must *disengage* from culture in order to *reengage* with a fresh voice.[8] Such disengagement is not an end in itself but a strategic matter for the sake of refocusing and redeciding about its identity and mission. In the context of failed Christendom where the church has become excessively accommodationist, accent must be placed on disengagement. But such sequencing of "disengagement/reengagement" is somewhat programmatic and theoretical, for in the real church on the ground, these twin strategies are worked at simultaneously. It is my own accent on disengagement to think that the church in the West must recover its baptismal nerve. It is, nonetheless, the burden of this chapter to consider reengagement, so that the afore-argued disengagement is seen to be strategic.

In the end it is the text and not contemporary interpretive categories that will most illuminate our question. In what follows I shall consider the actual textual practice of Israel. I do so to suggest that the rigorous either/or of "Chicago" and "Yale" is perhaps a peculiarly modernist trap that is not reflective of textual practice of Israel itself and therefore not finally our best guide. I shall want to consider the ways in which church talk always intends to be *public talk*, without ceasing to be *church talk*.

Cadences of Praise

I begin my exposition with Psalm 117, best known for being the briefest of all the psalms. Because it is brief, a great deal is assumed in its utterance, that is, its denseness is at first available only to the insiders. For all its briefness, however, the psalm contains most of what we need to consider concerning Israel as first addressee and others as second addressee:

> Praise the LORD, all you nations!
>   Extol him, all you peoples!
> For great is his steadfast love toward us,
>   and the faithfulness of the LORD endures forever.
> Praise the LORD!

The psalm proceeds in Israel's usual doxological pattern, a summons to praise and a reason for praise.[9] What interests us is the strange juxtaposition of this summons and this reason. The summons is stated in a two-line parallel with imperatives that mandate praise: "Praise, extol." The subject of the praise is explicit, "Praise Yahweh," praise the one known in the life, history, and recital of Israel. The one to be praised is the one known to the insiders, that is, the exiles. But the summons, as is characteristic, follows with a vocative, so that we know to whom the imperative summons is addressed:

> Praise Yahweh, all you nations,
> Extol him, all you peoples.

In its doxology, Israel invites, urges, summons, mandates the nations of the world to join in praise of Yahweh. We may imagine that this vocative surely includes the Babylonians, so that we may provisionally specify the urging of the exiles: "Praise the God of the exiles, you Babylonians." This is indeed a daring liturgical act, to dare to imagine that those from beyond Israel, who may even be hostile to Israel, could possibly join in praise of this God.

We could imagine, between the summons of verse 1 and the reason of verse 2, that the addressed nations and peoples who "overhear" the summons ask, with bewilderment, astonishment, and defiance: "Why should we praise your God, seeing that we have plenty of our own?" Why indeed! This is always the question that immediately follows the summons to praise.

It is to this implicit wonderment and protest that Israel gives its characteristic reason: This is why we mandate you to join us in praise:

> Because great is Yahweh's steadfast love toward us,
>   and the faithfulness of Yahweh endures forever.

The reason for praise is that Yahweh is a God of covenant loyalty (*ḥesed*) and utter reliability (*'emûnah*). That is the recurring ground for praise in Israel.

In issuing this reason for praise, Israel is honest. Great is Yahweh's *ḥesed toward us*, that is, toward Israel. Indeed, Israel's life and liturgical utterance are saturated with Yahweh's *ḥesed*. Already at Sinai, after the turmoil over the golden calf, Yahweh had provided for Israel grounds for life with Yahweh in a self-declaration:

> The LORD, the LORD,
> a God merciful and gracious,
> slow to anger,
> and abounding in steadfast love and faithfulness.
>   (Ex. 34:6b)

Since that utterance, moreover, Israel has discerned that all of its public life and all of its intimate life with Yahweh are a long, treasured sequence of Yahweh's *ḥesed*.

Indeed, Psalm 107, in a highly stylized way, offers four case studies of rescue—desert wanderings, gloomy prison, profound sickness, and even shipwreck. Each time Israel knows about miraculous rescue, and each time Israel is enjoined:

> Let them thank Yahweh for his steadfast love,
> for his wonderful works to humankind.
>   (Ps. 107:8, 15, 21, 31)

Or in a more specifically Israelite context, the highly stylized Psalm 136 has as a refrain after each plank of the recital of Israel's normative faith, ". . . for his *ḥesed* endures forever." All of life is seen in Israel to be a phenomenon of deep, abiding, unfailing fidelity. The exodus with all its violence is a show of *ḥesed* (vv. 10–15), the gift of the land with its imperialistic overtones is a sign of *ḥesed* (vv. 16–22). Israel is grateful and awed as it draws its identity close to the truth of Yahweh's *ḥesed*:

> It is he who remembered us in our low estate,
> for his *ḥesed* endures forever.
> And redeemed us from our foes,
> for his *ḥesed* endures forever.
>   (Ps. 136:23–24)

The provisional problem, however—surely noticed by the nations invited to join in praise—is that the data justifying praise is all so Israelite. Yahweh remembered *us*. He rescues *us*. He brought Israel out. He led his people through the wilderness. And even in Psalm 117, Israel asserts, "great is his *ḥesed* toward *us*."

The nations are to celebrate *ḥesed* given to Israel? Babylon should rejoice in how good Israel has known Yahweh to be? Not likely! Except—we may state the decisive "except" in two ways. First, Israel, in its doxological exuberance, is not able to contain *ḥesed* within the confines of Israel's life. Israel understands that *ḥesed* is the foundation of all of life. The life of the world, and of every human community, is sustained by Yahweh's fidelity. *Ḥesed* flows freely everywhere, through all of the domain of Yahweh, that is, through heaven and earth. So even in Psalm 136, Israel concludes beyond its own local credo:

> Who gives food to all flesh,
>> for his steadfast love endures forever.
>> (Ps. 136:25)

More important, in Psalm 107 the bid for thanks has four times as a refrain, "for his wonderful deeds (*nipl'ot*) to humankind (*bene 'adam*)," that is, to all humanity. Israel is able to notice, even in its doxological intensity, that the reality of Yahweh's *hesed* is not an Israelite possession, but it is a gift of Yahweh for all of Yahweh's creatures.

Israel, the first addressee of this proclamation, provides the specific details of the case study that grounds the doxology. But Israel, in its doxology, has no doubt that for those who know the "dense code" of Yahwism, that same *hesed* is elsewhere, everywhere generous, abundant, given to all, that is, to the second addressee.[10] That "dense code" of Yahwism is readily learnable outside Israel, because it codes in Yahwistic ways the most elemental realities of human life.

Moreover, Israel imagines and asserts that for all that the nations possess, for all the power, prestige, influence, and wealth that Babylon has, the irreducible reality that makes human life viable is *hesed*. That for which Babylon most yearns it can have only through the liturgical code of Yahwism. Israel's *hesed* sung about in this psalm is not a protected monopoly but a clue and a specific example of what is offered and may be given and celebrated everywhere.

Thus the nations, even those committed to the hegemony, are invited to praise the God of all *hesed* and *'emûnah* for the offer and gifts of loyalty and reliability that are everywhere on offer. But that on-offer gift, pervasive in Yahweh's governance, cannot be acknowledged, celebrated, or exulted in unless Babylon is able to say the word (*hesed*) and name the name (Yahweh). There is no hint in this doxological summons that Babylon is enjoined to become Israelite or to cease to be Babylon. The hymn is only an anticipation that even Babylon can join the song of *hesed* and *'emûnah* known in Israel's life and subsequently known in its own life.

But the invitation is insistent that Israel will offer, in addition to the substance of *hesed*, the source and agency of that *hesed*, the name of Yahweh, who is peculiar to Israel's life and must have seemed odd indeed to Babylon. What happens in this doxological process, perhaps not more than liturgical fiction but perhaps seriously anticipated event, is that the "us" of "great is his steadfast love to *us*" is expanded and recharacterized so that other peoples in their own cultures and idioms are also the joyful "us" who exude in a life saturated with Yahweh's *hesed* and *'emûnah*. In that reconstrual of "us" there is at least a chance that the public life of the empire will be transformed, not away from Babylon's true character, but away from Babylon's inappropriate, unacceptable, and now to be abandoned brutality.

Indeed, if the "us" of Psalm 117 is first Israel and then also belatedly Babylon, I may by extrapolation suggest that Nebuchadnezzar, the great and feared king of Babylon, is the paradigmatic second addressee. Nebuchadnezzar, according to the narrative, has been driven insane in his arrogant autonomy (Dan. 4:33). And then he is restored to sanity! He himself, the quintessential non-Israelite, can refer his life to the God of Israel:

> I, Nebuchadnezzar, lifted my eyes to heaven, and my reason returned to me.

> I blessed the Most High,
>   and praised and honored the one who lives forever.
> For his sovereignty is an everlasting sovereignty,
>   and his kingdom endures from generation to generation . . . .

> At that time my reason returned to me; and my majesty and splendor were restored to me for the glory of my kingdom . . .

> > for all his works are truth,
> >   and his ways are justice;
> > and he is able to bring low
> >   those who walk in pride.
>
> > (Dan. 4:34–37)

In Psalm 117, the second addressee is characteristically summoned in an imperative invitation. That invitation does not deny Israel's priority concerning the gift of ḥesed from Yahweh, but it acknowledges that Israel speaks no private rhetoric. Israel speaks a dialect that is open and available to all, because the offer of Yahweh is not a secret gift for the initiated, but is indeed an offer of the most concrete gift of humanness everywhere yearned for, everywhere required, everywhere given—acknowledged in Israel's daring, peculiar rhetoric without which the ḥesed of Yahweh is not known or acknowledged.

The preacher never ceases to focus upon the exilic community, that is, the first addressees who are the baptized. But you know how it is. On any given occasion of proclamation, there are others in the range of one's speaking. There may be informers who came only to report, but who are, against their better judgment, caught in the cadences of ḥesed.[11] There may be some who have the day off from intelligence work in the empire and come out of curiosity. There may be some who stumbled in and thought it was the train station. They listen not because they are taken with the peculiar name of Yahweh, but because they themselves know the parlance of ḥesed and yearn for 'emûnah. They sometimes notice that the good gifts of ḥesed and 'emûnah come with this peculiar name written all over them, for it is Yahweh's peculiar way in the empire, as it is among the exiles, to leave fingerprints of ḥesed and 'emûnah all about.

Cadences of Good News

The pivotal text for exiles in Israel, thoroughly saturated with the cadences of the Psalter, is Isaiah 40—55. For our purposes, there is no part of that text that is so crucial as the exultant declaration of 52:7 that, I have urged, is the taproot of evangelism and that provides a core model for the preaching task.[12] You know the text:

> How beautiful upon the mountains
> are the feet of the messenger
> who brings good news,
> who announces salvation,
> who says to Zion, "Your God reigns."
> (Isa. 52:7)

Now the reason I take this text as central for our concern is that it contains the double use of the term *mebassēr*, which is the earliest datable use of the word "message, messenger," with theological intentionality (see also Isa. 40:9–11). This is gospel news! It concerns the feet of *the gospel messenger*. This is the one who "messages" good to Israel. This text is a scenario in which a messenger has run from the place of combat between Yahweh and the gods of Babylon, who now brings news of the battle and its outcome to eager, expectant, waiting Jerusalem. The messenger comes with the message of Yahweh's victory. You can tell by the way he runs that the news is good. That is why his feet are "beautiful." He comes to Jerusalem and gives the outcome about which they had not known:

> Say to Zion, Your God reigns,
> Your God is king.
> Your God has just become king.[13]

Your God has defeated the gods of Babylon. The news is for Jerusalem, for Zion, for the waiting exiles who have for too long borne the burden of the empire.

And now, in response to the gospel announcement, there is celebration:

> Together they sing for joy . . . .
> Break forth together with singing,
> you ruins of Jerusalem;
> for the LORD has comforted his people,
> he has redeemed Jerusalem.
> (vv. 8–9)

The singing is a response to the declaration that the power of Babylonian might and the legitimacy of the Babylonian gods have been broken. The Jews in exile need no longer cringe and defer and obey. The world, the specific world of the exiles, has been turned toward freedom and well-being. The news sounds precisely like home! It is all very Israelite, very specific, very (if you will) ecclesial, very pro-exile and anti-empire, that is, very Lindbeckian!

The point I wish to make, however, puts a surprising twist on this ecclesial declaration that changes the world: "Your God is king!" It seems clear enough that the poetry of II Isaiah is not de novo. This poetry is permeated with the liturgical traditions of Israel and so I believe (with Mowinckel against Gunkel and Westermann) that the great enthronement formula of 52:7, so poignant in the specific context of sixth-century exile, is derived from and trades upon an older liturgical affirmation.[14]

I suggest, moreover, that the evangelical declaration of 52:7 is a localization for "Zion" of an older evangelical declaration situated in the enthronement festival of Jerusalem. Specifically, I suggest that it derives from something like Psalm 96. That psalm begins with six imperative summons to praise: "O sing, sing, sing, bless, tell, declare!" It is worth our noting that the fifth verb "tell" is "gospel (*bāśar*)," and that it is followed by a sixth verb that extrapolates the summons:

> Declare his glory among the nations,
>> his marvelous works (*nipl'ot*) among all the peoples.
>> (Ps. 96:3)

Note that the noun "marvelous works" is the same as the repeated term of Psalm 107 that is for "humanity." The Jerusalem liturgy exultantly imagines that the staggering good news of Yahweh is to be asserted among all peoples, among all nations, who need to know. It may be that the nations need to know, in order to be warned of the false loyalties that only bring death. Or it is possible that the nations must be told of the turn of cosmic government in order that they may sign on in joy for the new governance.

More specifically, in Psalm 96:10, the matter is put succinctly: "Say among the nations, 'Yahweh is king,'" that is, "Yahweh has just become king." The new role of Yahweh is a piece of data to be uttered in public. It is, moreover, good news. It is good news that the fraudulent government of the world is terminated. No wonder the heavens, the earth, the sea, the fields, and the trees sing for joy (vv. 10–13). Because the world will now be dealt with according to *'emûnah*, to utter reliability (the same word we have seen repeatedly in Psalm 107).

This exultant proclamation may have implicit within it Israelite aggrandizement. But that is not in any way expressed in the psalm. It is, rather, my suggestion that Psalm 96:10 is the older, more authoritative statement of the news, from which the subsequent, more specific assertion of Isaiah 52:7 is derived. Consider the following:

> Say among the nations, "Yahweh is king!" (Ps. 96:10)
> Say to Zion, "Your God is king!" (Isa. 52:7)

The first declaration is to the nations who now have the good news offered that the deathly loyalties they have long embraced are broken. The other gods are empty idols who do not warrant obedience and who can give no good gifts. This assertion in the psalm, we notice, is not from an explicitly Israelite perspective. It is not here "your God" who reigns; it is only Yahweh. It is Yahweh as Yahweh's sovereign self, at least here, without reference to Israel.

There is, to be sure, good contextual reason that the sweeping evangelical proclamation of Psalm 96:10 should be localized for Jewish exiles in Isaiah 52:7, in order to meet a quite specific need. Now the announcement is "say to Zion," not "to the nations." Now it is "your God," not "Yahweh." Surely the change intensifies the pertinence of the assurance given. The localized reformulation, however, surely does not reduce or limit or narrow the more normative evangelical proclamation of the psalm. Because it is here said "to Zion" does not cause it not to be said "to the nations." Because it is here "your God," it still is Yahweh who has Yahweh's own name, person, and purpose.

Thus I propose that the narrowed, more specific, more contexted assertion of Isaiah 52:7 is pastorally required, but the localized sounds do not for an instant eliminate the larger scope of the claim. Even in II Isaiah, what is said *to Zion* is said implicitly *to the nations*. What is said of "your God" is surely said by Second Isaiah of Yahweh the creator of heaven and earth. What is *explicitly localized* and Israelite is *implicitly large and comprehensive*. And therefore any Babylonian spy or official or curiosity-seeker present on the day of utterance is invited to recognize that what is true for this first addressee, an exile, is true for a second addressee, even Babylon.

It is odd indeed that the exilic community, so genuinely addressed, seeks to monopolize the news and fails to notice that the substance of the proclamation itself simply precludes any such narrow monopoly. The good news in which Israel rejoices is the good news in which all creatures and all nations may rejoice,

> For he is coming to judge the earth.
> He will judge the world with righteousness,
>   and the peoples with his truth.
>   (Ps. 96:13)

This coming, in the first instant, is no threat: It is good news, even to the Babylonians whose deepest yearning is for *'emûnah*, which is precisely the gift of this God of Israel who is the creator of the heavens and the earth. This of course is not our usual read on the gospel. But perhaps the failing is not in the ears of the nations who hear the gospel in narrowed ways, but in the utterance of the exiles, too much concerned to possess the news for themselves.

The Gospel for
the Second Addressee

If we take Psalm 96:10, "Say among the nations, 'Yahweh is king,'" as our beginning point concerning the "second addressee," that is, the world out beyond Israel, then we consider the Oracles Against the Nations as the place where Israel did indeed "say among the nations" concerning Yahweh. The Oracles Against the Nations constitute, in the several prophets, statements that are, on the face of it, addressed directly to the nations concerning the rule of Yahweh.[15] The oracles are, to be sure, an odd corpus in Old Testament literature and have been largely ignored in interpretive conversations concerning the "publics" of biblical address.

We may first of all ask to whom these oracles were addressed, given their ostensible address to the nations. It is easiest, and most commonly concluded, that the oracles were intended for the ears of Israel, to give salvific assurance to Israel. These oracles characteristically threaten the nations with judgment from Yahweh, and judgment upon the nations amounts to liberation for Israel whom the nations have oppressed. In this light, the Oracles function as a countertheme to the prophetic judgments against Israel.

If, however, we take the formal address of the oracles seriously, we cannot regard them simply as assurances to Israel, but may consider them as genuine address to the nations beyond Israel. Paul Raabe has suggested that the oracle is given in Israel but intended to be overheard by the nations.[16]

Seen in this way, the Oracles Against the Nations are indeed offered to "the second addressee" on the clear assumption that the "gospel of Yahweh" pertains not simply to Israel but to the public world in which Israel is embedded, and that "the news" of Yahweh is indeed "news" to which that world must attend. Raabe goes further with the "overhearing" to suggest quite concrete ways in which the contact between prophetic speakers and the nations might have transpired.[17] Such suggestions as those of Raabe are plausible, but highly speculative. I prefer to stay with the rhetorical intention of the oracles without engaging in such historical reconstructions.[18]

If in any case we imagine that such oracles were in some way intentionally addressed to and perhaps heard by "the second addressee," then we may ask, What is intended in such speech? What is the message this Israelite-Yahwistic speaker, thoroughly embedded in Israel's memory and rhetorical codes, wishes to speak to this "second public"? We may suggest three aspects to such a "gospel."

First, the message concerns Yahweh's sovereignty, splendor, and purpose, which must be honored. The first issue does not concern the destiny of the nations but *the glorification of Yahweh*.[19] That glorification, of course, takes place as the nations cease to mock and trivialize Yahweh and adhere to Yahweh. I may suggest two aspects of this honoring of Yahweh now "become king." One aspect is *the naming of Yahweh*, as though the nations must all become intentionally and explicitly Yahwistic. While there is some hint of this in the oracles, it is surely not a major accent. More important is *the doing of Yahweh*, that is, the *praxis* appropriate to Yahweh's character and rule.[20] This praxis means to forgo arrogance, autonomy, and brutality, and to be responsive to Yahweh's sovereignty and therefore to Yahweh's intention for *mercy and compassion*, not only toward Israel but toward other nations. The Yahwistic insistence is that the policies and practices of foreign nations should reflect the valuing of humanity, or as Israel regularly codes humanity, "widows, orphans, and sojourners." The gospel of Yahweh's kingship has direct and immediate insistences for socioeconomic, political, and military policy for every center of power, all of which are under the aegis of Yahweh.[21]

Second, derivative from the theme of the glorification of Yahweh, these oracles characteristically accent *judgment* upon those nations that defy Yahweh's intention and engage in praxis that is antithetical to that intention. Thus, for example, Ammon is condemned for having "ripped open pregnant women" (Amos 1:13), and Babylon for showing "no mercy" to Israel (Isa. 47:6). Indeed, the great preponderance of Oracles Against the Nations concern abuses of other peoples, especially Israel but not only Israel, which cannot be tolerated in a world where Yahweh is sovereign. Thus the judgment of Yahweh is the enforcement of Yahweh's nonnegotiable purposes over Yahweh's entire realm.[22]

Third, a minor note in these oracles also indicates that if a condemned nation repents, that is, changes policy and engages in Yahwistic praxis, the judgment of Yahweh may be revoked or reduced. Thus *a hope* is occasionally held out that if the offending nation acts in response to Yahweh's intention, that nation might indeed be spared judgment, given a second chance, and rehabilitated as a viable political enterprise.[23] This point should not be overstated, as it is indeed minimal. Insofar as it is voiced, it is congruent with the minimal hope the preexilic prophets offer to Israel and Judah, a minimal hope that is voiced in the midst of massive condemnation. Thus *for the nations as for Israel*, judgment is the preponderant accent, because Yahweh's rule cannot be taken lightly. But also for the nations as for Israel, there is an enduring chance that (a) the judgment will be averted, or (b) there will be new possibility after judgment. Charles Campbell has alerted me to the interesting possibility that the transformation of foreign powers to Yahwistic practice may be a parallel to and anticipation of the New Testament expectation that "the Principalities and Powers" may become obedient to the gospel.[24] What Israel discerned as its own true situation vis-à-vis Yahweh, it also understood as the true position of the nations vis-à-vis Yahweh. For the nations as for Israel, the reality of

Yahweh in the public domain bespeaks the derivative realities of judgment and hope.

It is important then to recognize that the horizon of "gospel" in the Old Testament is not confined to Israel, but looks well beyond Israel to the larger horizon of Yahweh's rule.[25] If we take Psalm 96:10 as the taproot of gospel to "the second addressee," and Isaiah 52:7 as its counterpoint gospel to "the first addressee," we may suggest that *Zion-Jerusalem-temple* constitutes the reference point for the gospel concerning both addressees. There is no doubt that Isaiah 52:7 concerns the bereft city of Jerusalem and/or its desperate citizens. There is also no doubt that the great enthronement psalms, including Psalm 96, have their primary setting in the Jerusalem temple.[26]

Thus the Jerusalem temple is the place from which Yahweh's Torah is offered to all nations (Isa. 2:1–5; Micah 4:1–5),[27] so that all nations have equal access, along with Israel, to the Torah, Yahweh's explicit intention for the world as for Israel. The insistence of Torah offered to the nations in Zion, moreover, is one of peace and justice wrought through disarmament, which is Yahweh's will for the world and which is the obligation of Israel and of the nations, who are now called to obey Yahweh, their rightful sovereign.[28] There is no doubt that Zion is the locus of Davidic dynastic imagination and thus deeply laden with ideological weight. It could hardly be otherwise, that is, the privileged position of Israel can hardly be doubted. At its best, however, as Ben Ollenburger urges, that privileged position is overridden in rhetoric that concerns Yahweh's intention for the nations without any reference to Israel.[29]

The convergence of *Yahweh's intention for the nations* and *Yahweh's intention for Israel* is perhaps best voiced in the "letter of Jeremiah" to the exilic community:

> But seek the welfare of the city where I have sent you into exile, and pray to Yahweh on its behalf, for in its welfare you will find your welfare. (Jer. 29:7)

There is for Israel no "separate peace," no private "welfare" by withdrawal from the world of international reality. This could perhaps be taken as common sense. It is, however, more than common sense. It is an insistence that Israel is a member of a larger community of nations over which Yahweh rules. Israel's future is in the midst of a Yahweh-practicing world community and not apart from it. For that reason, these unaccommodating witnesses to Yahweh adamantly insist that all members of that community—Israel and every other member—must attend to the news of the new Governance. It is the *doing* and not the *naming* of Yahweh that matters to these prophets.

The Second Addressee's Answers

The Oracles Against the Nations are highly stylized and schematic in their assertion of the gospel to the second addressee. As always in Israel's rhetoric, it is the narrative specificity that gives access to the schematic claims. For that reason, we may consider narrative accounts whereby "the second addressee" signals response to the gospel of Yahweh as a gospel beyond Israel.

1. The Exodus narrative (Exodus 1—15) is arranged so that painfully, little by little, Pharaoh comes to "know" and acknowledge Yahweh as ruler even of Pharaoh's Egyptian realm.[30] At the outset, Pharaoh defiantly dismisses Yahweh's imperative addressed to him:

> Who is the LORD, that I should heed him and let Israel go?
> I do not know the LORD, and I will not let Israel go. (Ex. 5:2)

Pharaoh refuses to *name Yahweh*, but also refuses to *practice Yahweh*, that is, to "let Israel go." Pharaoh, however, is worn down by the relentless sequence of plagues initiated by Yahweh, until he admits:

> This time I have sinned; the LORD is in the right (*ṣaddîq*); and I and my people are in the wrong (*rašaʿ*)! Pray to the LORD. (Ex. 9:27)

In the end, moreover, Pharaoh acknowledges that "the force" of blessing is with Yahweh:

> Take your flocks and your herds, as you have said, and be gone. And bring a blessing on me too! (Ex. 12:32)[31]

Indeed, the Exodus narrative serves to bring Pharaoh to an acknowledgment of Yahweh, who has "gotten glory over Pharaoh" (Ex. 14:4, 17).

2. In a different context, Jethro, the father-in-law of Moses, comes to acknowledge Yahweh:

> Blessed be the LORD who has delivered you from the Egyptians and from Pharaoh. Now I know that the LORD is greater than all gods, because he delivered the people from the Egyptians when they dealt arrogantly with them. (Ex. 18:10–11)

To be sure, in the scholarly discussion this confession of Jethro is all tied up in "the Midianite hypothesis" concerning the origins of Yahwism.[32] If, however, we take the text as is, it is Yahweh, evident in the life of Israel, who brings the priest of Midian to this confession of Yahweh. It is important, moreover, that Jethro's doxological affirmation concerning Yahweh comes to practical significance in the requirement of public leadership and public policy that is not self-serving, dishonest, or exploitative (v. 21). Such a practical requirement is implicit in the embrace of Yahweh, even for non-Israelites. The procedure is exactly congruent with the expectation of Psalm 117.

3. In the Joshua narrative of the taking of Jericho, Rahab, the social outsider, makes a public declaration of an acknowledgment of Yahweh:

> I know that the LORD has given you the land, and that dread of you has fallen on us, and that all the inhabitants of the land melt in fear before you. For we have heard how the LORD dried up the water of the Red Sea before you when you came out of Egypt, and what you did to the two kings of the Amorites that were beyond the Jordan, to Sihon and Og, who you utterly destroyed. As soon as we heard it, our hearts melted, and there was no courage left in any of us because of you. The LORD your God is indeed God in heaven above and on the earth below. (Josh. 2:9–11)

> We may believe that in such an assertion (and by Rahab's accompanying action on behalf of Israel) Rahab breaks with the naming of other gods and with the praxis of other gods who, in any case, worked to exclude her.[33]

4. In a later Joshua narrative, the Gibeonites won a political treaty of protection from Israel by a deceptive theological declaration:

> Your servants have come from a very far country, because of the name of the LORD your God; for we have heard a report of him, of all that he did in Egypt, and of all that he did to the two kings of the Amorites who were beyond the Jordan, King Sihon of Heshbon, and King Og of Bashan who lived in Ashtaroth. (Josh. 9:9–10)

To be sure, the confession is part of a strategem to deceive Israel into a covenant. Nevertheless, inside the narrative, the confession is heard and accepted by Joshua as credible (v. 15).

5. In the ark narrative the Philistines are portrayed as aware of Yahweh and respectful (fearful), even if not "converted" to Yahweh (1 Sam. 4:1–7:1). At the outset of the conflict between Israel and the Philistines, the enemies of Israel recognize the danger of Israel and the threat of Yahweh:

> Gods have come into the camp . . . Woe to us! For nothing like this has happened before. Woe to us! Who can deliver us from the power of these mighty gods? These are the gods who struck the Egyptians with every sort of plague in the wilderness. Take courage, and be men, O Philistines, in order not to become slaves to the Hebrews as they have been to you; be men and fight. (1 Sam. 4:7–9)

The Philistines understand the ominous implications for praxis in Yahwism, ironically presenting Yahweh as a God who enslaves. Thus the issue is not simply about naming God (as it never is), but about the practice of a rival

God. If we assume the hypothesis of "peasant revolt" or at any rate ground the Israelite movement in social reality, then clearly the Philistines are summoned not simply to *change the name* of God, but to *embrace covenantal, neighborly practices* that belong intrinsically to the name of Yahweh. Prior to the "ark narrative" in which the discourse is set (1 Sam. 4:1–7:1), the narrator has placed the "Song of Hannah" (1 Sam. 2:1–10), which sings about radical social transformation, the hungry and the full, the rich and the poor, and the needy who will sit with princes. The notice of 1 Samuel 22:1–2 suggests that issues of socioeconomic practices are never far removed from the Israelite movement, or from the horizon of the narrator. At the end of the narrative, a like acknowledgment of Yahweh as the God of the exodus leads to an altered Philistine policy toward the people of Yahweh:

> Why should you harden your hearts as the Egyptians and Pharaoh
> hardened their hearts? After he had made fools of them, did they
> not let the people go, and they departed? (1 Sam. 6:6)

The Philistines are not presented in the narrative as willing "believers" in Yahweh, but they nevertheless act in obedience to Yahweh, which is the most that the Oracles Against the Nations can in any case expect. When Dagon is defeated by the God of the exodus, issues of rich and poor cannot be long evaded.

6. In a very different context and idiom, Hiram the Phoenician responds to Yahweh as manifested in the wonders of the Solomonic enterprise:

> Blessed be the LORD today, who has given to David a wise son to
> be over this great people. (1 Kings 5:7)

The same response to Solomon is voiced by yet another non-Israelite, the Queen of Sheba:

> Blessed be the LORD your God, who had delighted in you and set
> you on the throne of Israel! Because the LORD loved Israel forever,
> he has made you king to execute *justice and righteousness*. (1 Kings
> 10:9)

It cannot be unimportant that this foreign ruler voices the precise, definitive Yahwistic terms, "justice and righteousness," the very qualities of public life that Solomon worked so hard to defeat. Thus we may imagine that in the ironic statement of the narrator, the foreigner is so grounded in Yahwism that she can witness to the Israelite king about matters of his true identity and warrant for royal office that he sought to deny. The utterance of this phrase, more ordinary on the lips of the prophetic tradition (Isa. 5:7; 9:7; Amos 5:7, 24; 6:12), evokes a heavy code for social practice, especially concerning the poor and the needy.

7. Naaman, the Syrian general, receives a healing from Yahweh and so responds in acknowledgment of Yahweh:

Now I know that there is no God in all the earth except in Israel.
(2 Kings 5:15)

To be sure, this is not exactly a recognition of the universal sovereignty of
Yahweh, for Naaman qualifies with "except in Israel." The subsequent narrative, moreover, shows Naaman seeking to transfer some of Yahweh's
"turf" back to Syria. Nonetheless, the narrative concerns a non-Israelite
embracing the rule of Yahweh, here a benign, healing rule.

8. Most spectacularly, in the Daniel narrative even Nebuchadnezzar, ruler
of Babylon and for much of the Old Testament a primary nemesis to Israel
and sometimes to Yahweh, makes a light acknowledgment of Yahweh:

> Blessed be the God of Shadrach, Meshach, and Abednego, who has
> sent his angel and delivered his servants who trusted in him. They
> disobeyed the king's command and yielded up their bodies rather
> than serve and worship any god except their own God. Therefore
> I make a decree: Any people, nation, or language that utters blas-
> phemy against the God of Shadrach, Meshach, and Abednego shall
> be torn limb from limb, and their houses laid in ruins; for there is
> no other god who is able to deliver in this way. (Dan. 3:28–29)

The concluding line of the decree is stunning indeed, for in the mouth of
Nebuchadnezzar is the assertion that "no other god," presumably including the gods of Nebuchadnezzar's own Babylonian hegemony, is able to
deliver (*naṣal*). Thus in a somewhat different idiom, Nebuchadnezzar reit-
erates the stylized recognition of Jethro, Rehab, and the Philistines. Each
of these foreigners makes the decisive point about Yahweh: not that Yahweh exists, nor that Yahweh is the only god that exists, but that Yahweh is
the one who can *deliver*. Thus, they echo Israel's own most elemental confession of Yahweh.

In Daniel 4, a parallel narrative portrays Nebuchadnezzar receiving
back his reason after a season of insanity (v. 34). What the narrative regards
as sanity is the full acknowledgment of the God of Israel, given in the very
cadences of doxology that are most Israelite:

> When that period [of sanity] was over, I, Nebuchadnezzar, lifted
> my eyes to heaven, and my reason returned to me.
>
> I blessed the Most High,
>   and praised and honored the one who lives forever.
> For his sovereignty is an everlasting sovereignty,
>   and his kingdom endures from generation to generation.
> All the inhabitants of the earth are accounted as nothing,
>   and he does what he wills with the host of heaven
>   and the inhabitants of the earth.

> There is no one who can stay his hand
> or say to him, "What are you doing?"
>   (Dan. 4:34–35)

Moreover, this affirmation in the mouth of this paradigmatic outsider concerns political praxis:

> Now I, Nebuchadnezzar, praise and extol and honor the King of
> heaven,
>
> > for all his works are truth,
> > and his ways are justice;
> > and he is able to bring low
> > those who walk in pride.
> >
> >   (Dan. 4:37)

It is worth noting that Nebuchadnezzar, in Daniel 4, does not "name the name," but only embraces the praxis that entails "truth" (*qšoṭ*) and "justice" (*dîn*) and precludes pride, which was the initial source of his insanity. And indeed, early in the king's transactions with Daniel, this Jewish witness asserted to the non-Jewish king:

> Atone for your sins with *righteousness*, and your iniquities with
> *mercy to the oppressed*. (Dan. 4:27)

Israel regularly offers its social vision and social burden to foreigners. The naming of the God of Israel here, "The Most High" (*'illay'*), is congruent with the affirmation of the King of Salem, another foreigner who also blessed "God Most High" (*'elyôn*) (Gen. 14:19).

I take this remarkable list of testimonies in the mouths of outsiders to Israel to be weighty evidence that "the second addressee" is summoned to alternative policy and conduct by the assertion of Yahweh's rule. This impressive list ranges all over the text, is expressed in a variety of genres, and no doubt serves a diversity of rhetorical intentions. We may observe that most of these responses to Yahweh are willing, glad, and grateful; in the cases of Pharaoh (Ex. 9:27; 12:32), the Philistines (1 Sam. 5:7–9; 6:6), and Nebuchadnezzar (Dan. 3:28–29), however, the response is forced upon the speaker by the sheer power of Yahweh. The reference point for Pharaoh, Jethro, Rahab, and the Gibeonites is *the Exodus memory*, whereas for Hiram and the queen of Sheba, it is *the splendor of the monarchy*. For Naaman, the persuasive ground for acknowledgment of Yahweh is *the personal transformation* of healing, and for Nebuchadnezzar it is a *public crisis of power*. In all of these various formulations, in any case, all of these "second addressees" are invited or required to enter the alternative world where Yahweh must be reckoned within practical and concrete ways. While the issues of practice are not uniformly present, they are characteristically expressed along with the naming of Yahweh. *The name* bespeaks *a transformative neighbor policy* of a most concrete kind. In most of these cases, the speaker, now brought to a new reality, joins in Israel's doxology, as anticipated in the summons of Psalm 117. In various ways, the outsiders have come to glimpses of Yahweh's *ḥesed* and *'amûnah* about which Israel sings, either through the same reality in their own lives or by observing these realities of well-being in Israel's life, which makes Israel safe from their onslaughts. The celebration of *steadfast love and faithfulness* characteristically issues in *justice and righteousness*. Embrace of Yahweh has within it inescapable neighbor mandates.

Conversion

These several cases give narrative specificity to the programmatic assumptions and concerns of the Oracles Against the Nations. What is clear in all of these examples is that there is a decisive *turn* on the part of the speaking subject, that is, a conversion and, we are led to believe, a new intention, a new perspective, and at least some of the time a new praxis. The "news" to the nations (Ps. 96:10) is as decisive for the nations as the news is decisive for Israel (Isa. 52:7)!

It is to be noted and insisted upon, however, that in most cases (perhaps the exceptions are Jethro and Rahab), this turn does not consist in becoming Israelite, that is, joining the covenant by undertaking life in the midst of Israel. In almost all of these examples, the speaking subjects are permitted and expected to remain in their appropriate sociopolitical contexts, with their long-standing, sociopolitical identities. Pharaoh remains an Egyptian; Nebuchadnezzar remains a Babylonian; the Gibeonites remain Gibeonites, and so forth.

Everything about these speaking subjects' context and identity is now changed by the profound reorientation of life around the central character of Yahweh who dominates the alternative narrative of reality. The narrative in each case, I propose, shows that prior to this Yahwistic acknowledgment, the speaking subject is alienated from the actual true self (political self) as given in a Yahwistic construal of reality. Thus Pharaoh is not able to be truly Pharaoh; Nebuchadnezzar is not fully able to exercise his rightful power. I use the term "alienated" to suggest that, mutatis mutandis, these non-Israelite speaking subjects are not unlike Israelite exiles, also alienated from their true life, that is, from their "true home."

The quintessential case is Nebuchadnezzar, profoundly *insane* in his alienated, arrogant, autonomous self (Daniel 4). The narrative of Nebuchadnezzar is centered not in the insanity but in the celebrated affirmation that "my reason returned to me." He is restored to sanity, to his true self, and so to his rightful power. The trigger for that return to sanity and rightful power, moreover, is his recognition that he is not autonomous, that is, his capacity to join gladly in the doxology of Israel to the God known primarily in Israel. The preferred narrative mode of articulation is to *worship other gods* and to *worship "the Most High."* That theological transformation surely carries with it a move from *exploitative social policy* to *an embrace of justice.* The rhetoric of the Old Testament makes clear that the greater the power that defies Yahweh, the greater is its brutalizing policy, that is, the more evidently *insane* is that power. This is a sobering reflection for those of us who read these texts as citizens of "the last superpower." A monopoly of power opens the way for *immense insanity* enacted as injustice, exploitation, and brutality.

Nebuchadnezzar, to be sure, is the extreme case. I do not suggest that all the outsiders are taken by Israel's narrative to be insane, but only that they are in some measure cut off from true self. I suggest that this insanity is marked by a grid of ABCs: Nebuchadnezzar and all of his ilk, living outside the Yahweh construal of reality, were governed by the following:

> *Autonomy,* in which the powers imagined they were on their own, not accountable to any, not protected by any, free for self. At least in the cases of Pharaoh and Nebuchadnezzar, such autonomy anticipates the verdict of Dostoyevsky, that "without God everything is possible." The "everything" about which Israel's texts care the most is the brutality that arises in such a world.
>
> *Arrogance,* embraced especially by Pharaoh and Nebuchadnezzar, who found it necessary for reasons of self-assertion and bravado public relations to boast and set themselves as rivals to other authority, including the authority of Yahweh (cf. Ezek. 28:2 and 29:3 for an articulation of such arrogance).
>
> *Anxiety,* perhaps best expressed in Pharaoh's madness, whereby he is obsessed with Israel, willing to destroy his beloved Nile (Ex. 1:22) and to let his own regime be destroyed (10:7) in order to punish and control Israel (destroying villages, in order to save them).
>
> *Brutality,* which is the sure fruit of autonomy, arrogance, and anxiety, which works not only against vulnerable Israel but against every other vulnerable community within the grasp of such power.
>
> *Covetousness,* enacted as rapacious economic policy, which leads to the trampling of others, their rights, and their property and an inordinate drive to control and possess, at whatever cost.

The conversion of the non-Israelites to the acknowledgment of Yahweh is in order to overcome the propensity to *insanity* that breeds *autonomy, arrogance, anxiety, brutality,* and *covetousness.* These non-Israelites do not need to become Israelites or perhaps not even adherents to Yahweh. They need only recognize that Yahweh, named and practiced, is the clue to a viable life in the world. The reception of sanity in a deeply crazed world is an agenda of covenantal, prophetic faith in the Old Testament. It is not different now. The gospel is an antidote to insanity expressed as public power. These narratives, concerned as they are with alienated *outsiders* in the same way that they concern the *insider* exiles of Israel, are about coming to true self, to true utterance, and to true power. The offer of the "news" is like coming home and ending the chaos of insanity. The homecoming that ends the chaos of insanity for non-Israelites is not unlike the homecoming that ends the chaos of exile for Israelites. There are not many offers of such sanity in the ancient world, nor are there many such offers in our contemporary world. The news of Yahweh is one such offer.

There is no doubt that Israel is privileged as the first addressee in preaching as generated by these texts. There is no doubt that the preacher first addresses the baptized community. It is, however, in my judgment, thoroughly unbiblical to settle for that first addressee. This news has a "second addressee" who finally awaits the same news as does the "first addressee." The church in much of the Western world, and surely in U.S. society, has lost its tongue for this second addressee. The preacher, in recovering this mandate and possibility, can still speak of *ḥesed* and *'emûnah* first in Israel with the inescapable consequence of justice and righteousness; at the same time, however, the nations are invited to receive and celebrate this offer of sanity, to celebrate the way Naaman did his healing and the way Nebuchadnezzar did his rehabilitation to power. Naaman could assert: "Now I know that there is no God in all the earth, except in Israel" (2 Kings 5:15). Clearly he became a changed Syrian general. Nebuchadnezzar could assert: "There is no one who can stay his hand or say to him, 'What are you doing?' " (Dan. 4:35). And he was, the narrator reports, a changed Babylonian ruler. 'Tis a gift to come down where you ought to be!

7

Rethinking Church Models through Scripture

To pose afresh the question of "models of the church" is itself an important matter. The question suggests a self-critical awareness that we are practitioners of a model that may not be the only or best one, and that other models of the church are indeed thinkable. Such a self-critical acknowledgment is a necessary awareness, if we are to do any "re-choosing" of our notion of the church.

The influential work of Avery Dulles's *Models of the Church* is a thoughtful reflection on the theme from a systematic perspective, and Paul Minear's *Images of the Church in the New Testament* has provided a shrewd summary of models of the church in the New Testament.[1] Both the works of Dulles and of Minear have come from their sustained involvement in ecumenism: Dulles in a series of bilateral conversations; Minear from his work in Faith and Order. Undoubtedly the most influential grid of models is that of Richard Niebuhr in *Christ and Culture*.[2] That presentation in my judgment, however, has been severely distorted by its many users. Niebuhr's study is a historical study that reflects on the way in which the church, in many different times and circumstances, has had to posture its life in various and different ways. In common usage, however, Niebuhr's typology has been taken as normative and has been dehistoricized. The result is that being less historically critical than Niebuhr himself, we are all agreed that "Christ transforming culture" is everywhere and always the normative mode of the life of the church. This amounts to a reductionism that fails to note that both in the Bible and in the history of the church, many other models and postures have been deemed not only necessary but required.

There is no single or normative model of church life. It is dangerous and distorting for the church to opt for an absolutist model that it insists upon in every circumstance. Moreover, we are more prone to engage in such reductionism if we do not keep alive a conversation concerning competing and conflicting models. Or to put it positively, models of the church must not be dictated by cultural reality, but they must be voiced and practiced in ways that take careful account of the particular time and circumstance into which God's people are called. Every model of the church must be critically contextual.

Posing the question about models in this way at this time requires us to think about "Christ and culture," to think about the place where God has put us and the appropriate modeling for our time and circumstance. It is my intention and hope that my exploration in the Old Testament will suggest larger lines of reflection and other characterization of the church far beyond the Old Testament. My reflection is in four parts: the Israelite monarchy, Israel before the monarchy, postexilic Israel, and from temple to text.

The Israelite Monarchy

In the center of the Old Testament, in the center literarily, historically, and theologically, is the Jerusalem establishment of monarchy and dynasty. It is the royal mode of Israel from David in 1000 B.C.E. to 587 B.C.E. that gives us the core model for the people of God in the Old Testament. This model dominates our thinking even as it dominates the text itself. It is this phase of Israel's life that provides the core of the time line around which we organize all of our thinking about the Old Testament. The test of that reality for me as an Old Testament teacher is that people regularly say, "Well, of course, the Old Testament model of faith and culture does not apply to us, because Israel is both state and church." That statement can only refer to the monarchical period, but it is thought to be "*the* model." In fact that convergence of "state and church" holds true for only a small part of the Old Testament, but it is the part that we take for granted and the part that dominates our interpretive imagination.

My thesis concerning this season in the life of ancient Israel is that as this model dominates our reading of the Old Testament, it has served well the interests of *an established, culturally legitimated church*.[3] I will identify four features of that model for the people of God:

1. There were visible, legitimated, acceptable, stable, well-financed religious structures with recognized, funded leadership. *The temple and its priesthood* played a legitimating role in the ordering of civil imagination, and the role of the stable temple for this model of church can hardly be overaccented.

2. There was civic leadership in *the role of the kings* that was at least publicly committed to the same theological discernment as was the stable religious structure of the temple. Indeed, the temple functioned as the "royal chapel." To be sure, the kings of Jerusalem were not so zealous as to enact

that theological discernment in concrete ways, except for Hezekiah and Josiah; however, they were at least pledged to it, so that a critical two-way conversation was formally possible. It did not seem odd for the priest to be in the palace, and it did not seem odd that the king should respond seriously to the finding of a temple scroll (cf. 2 Kings 22).

3. There arose in this model of the people of God an intelligentsia that was in part civic bureaucracy and in part the lobby of higher education. *The sapiential tradition*, the sages of the book of Proverbs who permeate and pervade the literature of the Old Testament, likely were influential in establishment thought in this period. This intellectual opinion accepted the formal presuppositions of temple religion; that is, the rule of Yahweh and the moral coherence of the world were assumptions of this community of reflection. This intelligentsia, however, exercised considerable freedom and imagination that drifted toward (a) autonomous reason and (b) support of state ideology.[4] Established religion thus served well the stabilization of power and knowledge for some at the expense of others.[5]

4. Exactly coterminous with stable temple leadership (priesthood) and with civic government that accepted the presuppositions of temple religion (king and sages) was the *witness of the prophets* who regularly voice a more passionate, more radical, and more "pure" vision of Israelite faith. It may indeed give us pause that the career of the prophets lasts only during the monarchy. That is, this voice of passion is viable only in a social circumstance where established powers are in principle committed to the same conversation.

This pattern of stable religious institution, sympathetic civic leadership, secularizing intelligentsia, and passionate prophecy all come to us as a cultural package. (I dare suggest that this is, mutatis mutandis, the governing model of modern, established Christianity in the West.) As is well known, this entire model in ancient Israel was swept away in a cultural-geopolitical upheaval. Moreover, the reason given for its being swept away is that the model had defaulted in its God-given vocation and was no longer acceptable to God.[6] Obviously I focus on this crisis because I believe we are in a moment of like cultural-geopolitical upheaval that undoes us personally and institutionally. That upheaval in our own time is jarring and displacing, and may be why we now reflect on alternative "models." It is worth noting that the collapse and failure of this model in 587 B.C.E. generated in ancient Israel enormous pluralism and vitality as the community quested about for new and viable models of life and faith.

Israel before the Monarchy

Happily, the temple-royal-prophetic model of the people of God is not the only model evident in the Old Testament. That mode was fitting and appropriate for a time of stable, established power. Israel as the people of God in the Old Testament, however, is not normatively a body of established power. Indeed, one can argue that such power as the Davidic monarchy had was a brief (400 years) passing episode, not to be again ever replicated in the life of this people of God.

Thus my second point is that Israel, prior to the time of David, did very well with another model of its life. If Moses is dated to 1250 B.C.E., then we may say that for the period from Moses to David, 1250–1000 B.C.E., Israel ordered its life and its faith very differently. Five characteristics may be identified for this model:

1. The life and faith of Israel lived and was nurtured and shaped by *the Exodus liturgy* that confessed that God called for moral, urgent, concrete disengagement from the power structures and perceptual patterns of the day (in this case Pharaoh, but later the Canaanite city-states), in order to be an alternative community. That liturgy regularly battled for the imagination of the community, which was vulnerable to seduction by the dominant social reality and which often succumbed. (Thus the perennial attraction of going back to the fleshpots of Egypt.) There is no way to soften or accommodate the sharp break that stands at the heart of Israel's self-identity, which must always be "re-nerved" for new situations of domestication. The community understands itself, so the liturgy attests, to be a community birthed in a radical and costly break.

2. *The meeting at Sinai* and *the endless process of reinterpretation of Torah* is an enterprise whereby Israel continues to think and rethink and rearticulate its faith and practice in light of its liberation. That practice required endless adjudication among conflicting opinions. If we take Leviticus to be more or less conservative and Deuteronomy to be more or less radical, then the ongoing tension between Leviticus and Deuteronomy already sets the guidelines and perimeters for policy adjudication that is still required of us.[7] This continued Torah interpretation exhibits the church seeking to discern the mind and heart of God. It is only agreed that this community (a) is shaped in something like a holy covenant, (b) is a community liberated by God for new life in the world, and (c) refuses the sustenance of Pharaoh. All else remained and remains to be decided.

3. Early Israel from 1250 B.C.E. to 1000 B.C.E. had none of the features outlined above for the period of the establishment. It had no stable institutions; no sympathetic, stable civic leadership; no secularizing intelligentsia; and no prophetic voice. Imagine Israel without temple, without king, without sages, without prophets! That is how it was. Early Israel had much more modest means and modes. Indeed, Israel in this period had *to make up everything as it went along*. It was a community that had to improvise. Its daring, risky improvisation can, on the one hand, be seen as a practice of *enormous borrowing* from the culture around it. On the other hand,

this was a process of *deep transformation* of what was borrowed, transformed according to Israel's central passion for liberation and for covenant.

4. Unlike Israel in the monarchical period, Israel in this early period was not unified, or we may say, not rigorously "connectional." It was, as the sociologists say, *a segmented community* of extended family units and tribes. These units had no central authority or treasury, nor were they blood units. They were communities bound by a common commitment to its central story and its distinctive social passion. It is fair to say that the story of liberation and covenant was inordinately important, but it became much less important in the period of establishment when the temple made the story less palpable and less urgent. In the early period, lacking visible props, the community depended on the story being regularly heard and told.[8]

5. The community of early Israel was a community that was socioeconomically marginal. Its central metaphor is either the "wilderness" or the occupation of marginal land that no one else wanted. In the "wilderness," the community lived by bread from heaven and water from rock, without guaranteed or managed resources. In its marginal land, it depended in its times of threat on the move of the spirit to give energy, courage, and power sufficient for the crisis. This was a community that lacked the capacity (or perhaps the will) for more stable resources but managed by a different posture of faith and witness.

I suggest then that in the most radical way possible, Israel was indeed *a new church start*. A new church start here means the planting of an alternative community among people who were ready for risk and who shunned established social relations because such resources and patterns inevitably led to domestication and to bondage. It is a new church start that specialized in neighbor priorities and that had at its center the powerful voice of Moses—and Joshua—and Samuel, whose main work is voicing and revoicing and voicing again the liturgy of liberation and the covenant of reshaping communal life, power, and vision.

It may give us pause that the temple model grew increasingly impatient with the voice of Moses, whose leadership was kept in endless jeopardy and under abrasive challenge. It is likely that the narrative of the Golden Calf (Exodus 32), wherein Moses rebukes Aaron, is a partisan assault made by the "new church start" model against the established church model that is too busy generating structure and icon.

Postexilic Israel

At the other end of the Old Testament, we may identify yet another model for the community of faith. The temple model came to an abrupt end in 587 B.C.E. To be sure, there was a second temple built after 520 B.C.E., but it never came to exercise a dominant place in the community, nor to capture the imagination of subsequent interpreters. Clearly with the events of 587 B.C.E., the symbiotic relation of king and prophet collapsed. This new circumstance began in exile under the Babylonians and then continued under the patronage of the Persians and finally faced the coming of Hellenization. It is worth noting that characteristically, Christians know very little about this period, pay little attention to it, and care little for it. Very likely this lack of interest reflects our stereotypes of "postexilic Judaism," which go back at least to the caricatures of Julius Wellhausen. Our systemic neglect reflects the anti-Semitic tendency of our interpretive categories. There is at the present time great attention to this period among scholars that requires us to move well beyond our dismissive stereotypes. Recent scholarship suggests that there was a greatly variegated practice of Judaism bespeaking pluralism in this period. It was a pluralism that was theologically serious, with enormous imagination in its practice of faith and vitality in its literary inventiveness.

My suggestion is that this exilic, postexilic period after the collapse of the temple hegemony is one to which we must pay considerable attention, for it may, mutatis mutandis, be echoed in our own time and circumstance. Three facets of this model may be noted:

1. The community of faith had to live in a context where it exercised *little influence over public policy*. It is debatable the extent to which the imperial overlords exercised benign neglect so long as they received tax payments, and the extent to which they were hostile in an attempt to nullify the scandalous particularity of the Jews. The stereotype we have is that the Babylonians were hostile and the Persians were benign, but that may be an ideological construct put together by those indentured to the Persian government. In any case, after one considers the drama of Elijah versus Ahab, Amos versus Amaziah, and Jeremiah versus Zedekiah, one notices that there is no such confrontation model now available. The reason is, I submit, that there is no one on the side of power interested in such a confrontation, for this community of faith had become politically innocuous and irrelevant.

2. The *temptations to cultural syncretism* and the disappearance of a distinct identity were acute, particularly in the Hellenistic period. The Maccabean period offers us an example of Jewish boys who were embarrassed about their circumcision and who tried to "pass." In the monarchical period, while there was indeed syncretism, there was no danger of losing an Israelite identity, because public institutions supported that identity, and one could afford to be indolent about it. Now, because such institutions are lacking, and because the pattern of social payouts tended to invite people away from this community of peculiar identity and passion, the deliberate maintenance of a distinctive identity required great intentionality.

3. In the face of political irrelevance and social syncretism, a main task

of the community was to work very hard and intentionally at the cultural-linguistic infrastructure of the community.[9] Daniel L. Smith has called that work the development of *strategies and mechanisms for survival*, because the threat was in fact the disappearance of the community of faith into a universalizing culture that was partly hostile to any particularity and that was partly indifferent.[10] Among these strategies for survival, three seem crucial for our reflection.

First, this community, in the face of sociopolitical marginality, worked at the *recovery of memory and rootage and connectedness*. The primary evidence of this in the Old Testament are the extended genealogies, most of which are articulated in this later period. The purpose of genealogy is to connect the threatened present generation with the horizon of reference points from the past. A studied recovery of the past intends to combat the "now generation," and the disease of autonomy and individualism that imagines that we live in a historical vacuum.

A second strategy for survival in a community at the brink of despair is the *intense practice of hope*. The rhetoric of the community filled its imagination with the quite concrete promises of God. In its extreme form, this rhetoric of hope issues in apocalyptic. In our study of apocalyptic, there is much for us to learn about the sociology of our knowledge. When the church is safe and settled and allied with the status quo, it is impatient with apocalyptic. Indeed, most critical scholarship has dismissed apocalyptic as "bizarre." Among the communities of the marginal, however, who find the present laden with hopelessness, apocalyptic is a rhetorical act of power. Thus this literature and this rhetoric belong rightly on the lips of the "world weary" who see this rhetoric as critically subversive of every status quo. It is telling now that apocalyptic rhetoric in our culture appeals to apparently well-off people who are beset by despair.

I believe this is important because satiated young people in the United States (including some of our own children) mostly do not know that something else is yet promised by God. That future is not to be wrought by our busy, educated hands, but by the faithfulness of God. The community at the margin, when it functions at all, is a community of intense, trustful waiting.

The third strategy of survival worth noting is that the postexilic community became *an intensely textual community*. It was busy formulating the text, so it is widely believed that the period around the exile is precisely the period of canonization, the making of normative literature. It was also busy interpreting the text. This is the period of the emergence of *the synagogue*, which is the place of the text, the formation of *the Beth Midrash*, "house of study," and eventually, the appearance of *the rabbis* who are teachers of the tradition. Textual study was focused on the imaginative construal of a normative text. This imaginative construal of the text that so characterizes

Judaism did not drive toward theological settlement or moral consensus but believed that the act of construal of this text itself is a quintessential Jewish act. Such an act in the midst of marginality did not need a controlled outcome.

With a high and passionate view of scripture, we must not miss the point concerning social power. The point of sustained textual study is not objective erudition, information, or conclusion. The point is rather to enter into and engage with a tradition of speech, reflection, discernment, and imagination that will prevail over the textual constraints of Persian power and Hellenistic hostility. A textless Jew is no Jew at all, sure to be co-opted and sure to disappear into the woodwork. And my sense is that a textless church is increasingly no church at all.

The *New Yorker*, of all places, has suggested that the United States has had as its organizing story "The Cold War."[11] That story has now failed and our civil community, says the *New Yorker*, is essentially "storyless." So it has always been; the story offered by the dominant empire turns out to be no story at all. These besieged Jews knew that. They knew not only that to keep their young they had to engage the text on its own terms. They also dared to imagine that their particular text was the voice of God among them, and the voice of a true story that would persist in the face of empire and cultural hegemony. This community developed a deep and vibrant confidence in its text, which is what the process of canonization is all about.

Thus it is my conclusion that circumstance required a shift *from a temple-royal-prophetic community to a textual community* that struggled with the text in all its truth and in all its dangerous subversiveness, continually witnessing to another mode of reality.

Beginning Again
from Old Memories

I have suggested three models that are intensely reflective of social crisis and historical circumstance:

    a.   Premonarchical model as *"new church start."*
    b.   Monarchical model as *temple community.*
    c.   Postexilic model as a *textual community.*

It is readily clear that the early premonarchal and the last postmonarchal have more in common, and both are easily contrasted with the security and stability of the monarchal model. Finally then, we may reflect on the *dialectic relation of early and late models* that had so much in common.

There is no doubt, on the one hand, that the late community went back to the early community. It in fact jumped over the monarchical period to find resources in the early sources that could sustain it. It did not find in the period of the establishment what it needed, but was driven back to more primitive and less stable models. This is poignantly evident in Ezra, the founder of Judaism, who is the second Moses and who replicated the first Moses.

On the other hand, however, and much more delicately, the late community not only used the early materials but intruded upon those materials, and preempted and reshaped the early tradition for its own use. In the documentary hypothesis concerning the Pentateuch, the Priestly tradition represents a later recasting of early tradition. The late material is not all in the late part of the Bible, but some of the later material is cast as early material. As you may recall, the Priestly tradition is conventionally dated to the sixth or fifth century, either exilic or early postexilic. Thus when we read the pre-David texts, if we pay attention, many of those texts are postexilic and show not only the needs but also the faith of the later community. Four quick examples demonstrate late material cast as early material:

1. *Genesis 1:1–2:4a* on the creation is a P statement that culminates in Sabbath as a sacrament. It is in the late period that Sabbath emerges as a mark of Jewishness, when the Jews in an alien environment had to assert that Jews (and others) were not cogs in any imperial machine but creatures made in God's image, destined for dignity. Thus the late liturgy responded to a social situation of despair by generating a sacrament of dignity and liberation.

2. *Genesis 17*, in which Abraham circumcises his offspring, is a Priestly document, asserting in the late period that the community must have a visible discipline of identity. Circumcision, albeit sexist, is a visible mark whereby insiders can be distinguished from outsiders, so that members of the community know who was marked by God's promise and who stood under God's commandment. Circumcision emerged in the postexilic period as a decisive mark of Jewishness. Such a text in such a community invites a rethink of the marking of baptism in a society that is either hostile or neglectful.

3. *Exodus 16*, the story of manna in the wilderness, contains Priestly elements. The wilderness becomes, in such a story, a cipher for exile, so that the exiles, marginated faithful people, live by the gifts of God and not by their managed surplus. It is striking that the text warns against surplus, the kind of surplus that made the temple possible. Moreover, the text relentlessly culminates in Sabbath, the occasion when an abundance of food is given. (See Isa. 55:1–3 and Daniel 1.)

4. *Exodus 26* is a design for the tabernacle in a Priestly tradi-
    tion. While the model for the tabernacle no doubt reflects
    the temple, the intent of the text is to permit God mobility,
    capability of being on the way with God's displaced people.
    This is a God who has a portable shrine and will travel.

The point of this linkage of late and early is to suggest that in doing textual work (which became a primary activity of the marginated community),
the late community must recast what the early community had done for the
sake of its own crisis. This means that after the establishment, as before the
establishment, this was essentially a "new church start." Postexilic Judaism
is a vibrant act of new generativity, not enslaved to its oldest memories, and
not immobilized by its recent memory of establishment power. Ezra is the
great "new church start" leader. A new church start means reformulating
the faith in radical ways in the midst of a community that has to begin again.
For Ezra as for Moses, new church starts do not aim at strategies for success, but at strategies for survival of an alternative community. What must
survive is not simply the physical community; what must survive is an alternative community with an alternative memory and an alternative social perception rooted in a peculiar text that is identified by a peculiar genealogy
and signed by peculiar sacraments, by peculiar people not excessively be-
holden to the empire and not lusting after domestication into the empire.

From Temple to Text

Whether this grid is pertinent to our present rethinking partly depends
on the cogency of the analysis offered of these traditions. It also depends
partly on a judgment about whether we are in a time when our alliance with
the dominant culture is being broken, whether the power of the temple is
broken, whether the empire is indifferent or hostile, whether the prophets
lack a partner in confrontation. This argument receives support from three
sources at least:

1. The collapse of modernity is a crucial theme in much con-
    temporary social analysis.[12] We have to face that our domi-
    nant models of church have been fashioned for modernity
    and depend on its presuppositions, presuppositions which
    no longer prevail.
2. It is clear that conventional kinds of theological speech are
    no longer accepted as "public speech." Civic leadership is
    not in any serious way formally committed any longer to es-
    tablished church rhetoric, so appeals from our tradition are
    less and less significant politically.

3.   Many of our young (particularly the young of good liberals, but not only the children of liberals) have only the vaguest idea of what we intend in our faith.

A move *from temple to text*, a move that I have stated in the boldest form, requires a reconsideration of our social location, of the resources on which we can and must count, and the work we have to do about the infrastructure that has largely collapsed. While we may find wilderness-exile models less congenial, there is no biblical evidence that the God of the Bible cringes at the prospect of this community being one of wilderness and exile. Indeed this God resisted the temple in any case (cf. 2 Sam. 7:4–7). In the end, it is God and not the Babylonians who terminated the temple project. In the face of that possible eventuality in our own time and circumstance, the ways for the survival of an alternative imagination in an alternative community call for new strategies.

8

Disciplines of Readiness

The journey of Christians to this time and place has been a long, odd journey, and now comes a moment's resting place, and a new beginning. In my comments, I will consider first that long journey, and then the new beginning.

Israel's Journey

God's people, so the Bible claims, is a people on the way. There are strange connections and parallels between the biblical narrative travel and our Christian narrative of coming to this time and place. It would be possible to read our journey in other ways. I propose for now, however, that we read our travels together in light of that older biblical story we take as normative.

The biblical account of a faith journey is set in three large stages, stages that may be a clue to our own life:

1. The beginnings of that story, voiced already in Genesis and Exodus, are of a people deeply at risk, without home, without land, without security, moving in trust to a new place. No doubt they travel for many reasons—to escape oppression, to acquire new land, to enter a fresh prosperity, to have a zone of freedom and power in their life. Mostly, however, as the story is told, this traveling people is summoned and sent by *the sovereign promise of God*. It is the voice of God that initiates the journey. This is a God who notices trouble, who promises to accompany, who anticipates blessing and well-being, who drools and dreams with Israel over milk and honey. In the presence of that sovereign promise, Israel is deeply certain that bondage, barrenness, oppression, and marginality are not God's will for them—or for any one.

2. As the biblical story goes, the promise of God is kept. The land is reached and acquired. The second stage of this sweeping narrative concerns

Israel in the land. God is faithful. Israel did come to the wondrous land of milk and honey, cities and cisterns, vineyards and olive trees and bronze and iron (Deut. 6:10–11). Israel no longer needed manna; now the Israelites ate the produce of the good and generous land (Josh. 5:11–12).

The land, however, decisively transformed Israel. The land seduced Israel, until the Israelites wanted more and more of land and security and goods. They organized great cities, great armies, and great tax systems; they ate well, exceedingly well at the expense of the others (1 Kings 4:22–28). In the end, Israel forgot (see Deut. 8:11–19). They forgot that this good life and this good land were gifts, the outcome of God's promise. Greed overcame gratitude, selfishness displaced compassion. Covenant was reduced to control and exploitation. They forgot, and they imagined that their might and the power of their hand had gotten them this wealth (Deut. 8:17).

In their self-sufficiency Israel encountered *the sovereign demand of God*. It was a demand on the lips of the prophets; it was also a demand that became visible and inescapable in the concrete processes of economics and politics. The demand was that power must be administered in new ways. Power must be held within the fabric of human, social transactions. Israel learned, repeatedly, reluctantly, painfully, that God had not abdicated. In the end, mismanaged power would hurt and destroy, mismanaged land would be lost, mismanaged security would evaporate, and mismanaged promises would fail. The Israelites learned that they could not presume upon God, because among the prosperous and secure, the bite of God's demand is more forceful than the surge of God's promise.

3. Israel had entered the land with buoyancy. Now Israel left the land disconsolate, like mother Rachel, refusing to be comforted (Jer. 31:15). The third stage of this awesome tale is one of land loss, displacement, and exile. The Israelites thought exile could not happen to them; now, as the tale winds down, they are as bereft as the old slaves in Egypt and the old, barren mothers in Genesis.

It is difficult to determine how the exile happened. A case can be made that the defeat was simply a result of failed leadership in the presence of the expansionist imperial policies of Babylon. The whole sorry outcome can be explained on the basis of such surface facts. That would be enough of an explanation, except that Israel is endlessly haunted by the hard, shrill, uncompromising words of the prophets, who see beforehand and who speak outside the rhetoric and rationality of the dominant culture. They speak "woe" and "therefore" and assert that Israel's life is shaped by a purpose other than its own, that life has a moral coherence that cannot be mocked. Israel never doubted that its exile is a theological happening.

There is a departure and a displacement; there is a city left behind and now life in a hostile, alien environment. The economic–political realities were hard enough to bear. Through these circumstances, Israel came to meet *the sovereign absence of God*. The glory had indeed departed (see 1 Sam. 5:21–22; Ezek. 9:3; 10:4–5). The poet pounds the point: "None to comfort, none to comfort, none to comfort" (Lam. 1:2, 9, 16, 17, 21). No God, no presence, and life has failed because God had been mocked. Israel is left hopeless and helpless, without energy or buoyancy, barely going through the motions, ready to abandon its failed identity.

Chronologically, Israel's story is a long history, filled with odd gifts. Theologically, however, that long story is encapsulated in a few lean formulae: *sovereign promise, sovereign demand, sovereign absence*, so much given, so quickly lost. This community arrives at a point in its journey where it is as it began. It began bereft, barren, powerless, without hope in the world. Now in exile it has become once again what it was in the beginning: bereft, barren, powerless, without hope in the world. This community in exile is as barren as Sarah, as oppressed as Moses. There may be more to come. There may be a fresh summons to faith issued by God. There may be a new, daring adventure in theological creativity. There may be a new season of life and faith. At this moment, however, there is only waiting and grieving and wondering. This may be an end, but Israel hopes otherwise. Israel hopes, but does not know.

That narrative account, of course, is too sweeping. There are many historical-critical problems with it. Nonetheless, it catches the canonical claim about our people. For our purposes the main point is that this journey is a journey with reference to the power, purpose, and presence of a very particular God. There is for Israel no journey without this God, but this God insists that the journey be one of a very specific kind, a journey of risk, trust, and obedience. That insistence does not mesh easily with our predilection to have the journey on our own terms. And the journey on our own terms ends in disaster.

The American Journey

Consider what happens if we reread our own journey to this time and place in light of that biblical narrative. Ours is not the same journey, and the parallels should not be forced. Ours is a different journey, different mainly because it is ours, different because it is modern, more knowing, more an exercise in self-direction, more secular, more on our own terms. Yet we hear in our journey some of the same wondrous, costly accents.

Consider our tale in three stages, albeit too schematically. I tell the story from the perspective of white Europeans, because that has been the dominant and dominating story line among us. I am aware that others have other story lines; the truth is, however, that those others have all had to accommodate themselves and their stories to this white-European narrative.

American Indians have had to accommodate by surrendering their land and their power. Black Africans have had to surrender much of their story in subservience, in order to service the white-European story line. Asians have stayed marginal and have only of late been admitted into the story at all. Therefore in this telling I do not exclude them but simply observe how many people have paid deeply in order to make the main story "work" at all.

1. That story, the white-European story, became as it evolved an American story, a story of moving to a new land for all kinds of mixed reasons, for escape from bad situations, for religious freedom, because of entrepreneurial ambition. The rhetoric that dominated the arrival in the new land was the rhetoric of sovereign promise, of God leading, willing, and guiding. There is a fairly straight line from "a city set on a hill" to "manifest destiny" to being "leader of the free world." It was not doubted then and it is not doubted now that God's providential care has guided this new establishment, which is passionately theological and intensely political. In making the new establishment, we were no more troubled about preempting the land than were the Israelites, because the socio-political realities were militantly reread according to a self-serving theological passion.

2. The second stage of this American story is the incredible account of American prosperity and expansionism and the development of tax systems, defense systems, and welfare systems. An American Empire emerged that exploited markets, established larger spheres of influence, and regarded the "underdeveloped" world as our rightful domain, a proper sphere for the missionary work of Americanism.

In ancient Israel, Solomon built a legitimating temple to give divine blessing to the new concentration of wealth and power. The American enterprise never arrived at a national temple, but we did arrive at a national rhetoric that is in large measure a Presbyterian rhetoric. It is the Presbyterian theological tradition—certainly not the tradition of Roman Catholicism or Lutheranism or frontier sectarianism—that established the rhetoric of legitimacy and let Presbyterians believe that their expanding economy and their self-serving ideology were a delight to God. As the temple served the king in ancient Israel, so the Presbyterian religion was largely at peace with the exploitative mercantilism that used up people for the sake of economic growth and national security.

That season of convinced intensity had its price, to be sure. That perception of American destiny was an odd mixture of compassion and impatience, of inclusiveness and insensitivity. In the long run, impatience outran compassion, and insensitivity overrode inclusiveness. Our public institutions are mainly shaped to serve the center and neglect the margin. There has been a growing insensitivity about the excluded who do not share in the economic miracle that God has wrought among us, the miracle "of houses which we did not build and vineyards which we did not plant and cisterns which we did not hew."

This long period of uncriticized theological legitimacy is not without its shrill poets of dissonance. There are voices of marginality that speak of common access and dignity and political rights. There are occasional fits and starts of societal reform, of labor rights and voters' rights and civil rights and human rights. Our society, however, is not excessively hospitable to such voices. The engines of prosperity and security have found ways of discounting such marginal realities and leaving such poets of dissonance unnoticed. And when they are unnoticed, our capacity for not noticing only grows larger. We are caught in the staggering act of giving theological legitimacy to that which contradicts our faith. The demands of God for justice and inclusion and caring are muted. Only now are we learning that those demands are not so easily eliminated as we had imagined.

3. Perhaps we now live in stage three of this second narrative. There has been no great deportation or displacement of persons to match the experience of ancient Israel. Scholars, however, think that there was not such a great deportation in ancient Israel either. The exile is a dramatic, liturgical event of marginality, alienation, and displacement. The exile may indeed be happening in our white Christian-American world without our even noticing. The work of exile among us need not be a big, dramatic event caused by the communists, but may come unnoticed and unacknowledged. Exile may take the form of brutality, indifference, cynicism, and despair, showing up in drug abuse and child abuse and wife abuse— endless abuse. All the while, the fabric of human care, human dignity, and human possibility is destroyed in the powerful name of greed, as though the American dream has run its course and nobody knows what to do, or even when to notice.

We religionists are caught in an odd endorsing and legitimating, when in our knowing, we may want to talk about the sovereign absence of God, an absence evident in the secularization of a society that seems to manage very well by itself. And in an unconvincing religious recovery that lacks credibility and substance, we sense ourselves ever more distant from old forms and old practices. The rhetoric sounds less convincing, and we know that the real decisions are increasingly made on other grounds. We scarcely have any poets left whose lips tremble enough to speak our truth for us. We sense the absence, an absence evident in the vacuous rhetoric of our national leaders who still work their weary timidity from the old narrative in ways no longer credible. We stand, I imagine, at the bitter, lonesome, tail end of a narrative nearly powerless, largely used up.

God's Gift of Newness

I have reviewed these histories because I want to reflect with you on the theme of exile as the locus of this new beginning. In ancient Israel the exile is an overwhelming reference point for faith. Exile is the decisive event in the Old Testament for faith as for history. The notion of exile is initially geographical. It suggests physical dislocation. Exile, however, is not primarily geographical. It is a cultural, liturgical, spiritual condition; it is an awareness that one is in a hostile, alien environment where the predominant temptation is assimilation, that is, to accept and conform to the dominant values that are incongruent with one's faith and destiny. The alternative to assimilation is despair, to yearn for nonbeing, because one's situation is indeed hopeless and helpless.

Two things about exile in ancient Israel make it useful as an organizing metaphor for our own experience. First, exile is largely paradigm and model, not an extensive historical fact. Though not everyone was deported, all Jews, then and subsequently, participated in the sense of being exiles, lived between assimilation and despair, and were summoned to fresh faith. Exile became a definitional mark of this community of faith for all the generations to come.

Second, the situation of exile created an enormous theological crisis in Israel and evoked astonishing theological creativity. The crisis emerged because God's absence suggested God's defeat, failure, and infidelity. In response, in exile Judaism was birthed and the canonical literature of the Bible was decisively shaped. Our Old Testament is a theological attempt to stay faithful in exile when the old narrative of faith has exhausted itself in disobedience. Judaism and the tradition that produced our faith emerged in exile because Jewish exiles resisted both assimilation and despair. Using this model, I shall argue that it is now our theological vocation, when our story has run out, to resist our own assimilation and despair.

With the use of the metaphor of exile I affirm that we find ourselves in a cultural context in which our central faith claims are increasingly unwelcome and are received, if not with hostility, at least with indifference. We find ourselves alienated from the dominant value system. That is why I have insisted that exile is not primarily a geographical phenomenon but a liturgical, cultural, spiritual condition; one may indeed be an exile while being geographically at home.

It may seem to you that this metaphor is inappropriate, because in many places Christians are in places of power and influence and are not marginal. That is surely correct. Those persons, however, find out even in their power and influence how difficult it is to act through the rhetoric and out of the claims of this theological tradition. Like Daniel and the exiles of ancient Israel, the powerful among us must travel mostly incognito in the culture at large. The rhetoric of our public community has largely shifted, and our speech, long the dominant public rhetoric of our society, is now odd and alien. We are told that "mainline" churches have lost their central place in public discernment. We may be permitted our rhetoric, but no one expects the public conversation any longer to be cast in our terms.

The more difficult part is the recognition that the faith claims (as distinct from rhetoric) in our theological tradition are increasingly at odds with dominant American values. This is a new situation for us. It has come about not because the faith has grown more radical but because the anti-human side of American self-discernment has grown more powerful and bold. Thus as we make this new beginning it is important to recognize our true situation. We hold to an identity and a vocation, an overriding loyalty, that is largely unwelcome in our society.

The question this leaves for us is how to embrace our exile when we sense God's absence, how to respond in faithful ways to such an odd circumstance. I have already suggested that three lines of response are possible.

1. It is possible to respond in *assimilation*. There were a number of Jews in Babylon who found Jewishness too demanding, and who capitulated and simply joined dominant Babylonian values and identity. It is possible for baptized Christians to assimilate into imperial America in the same way, to embrace the dominant American hopes and fears that are all around us, to live so that the world does not notice our odd baptism or our odd identity.

2. It is possible to respond in *despair*. We can recognize the power of Babylon and the absence of Yahweh, concluding that this situation of homelessness and displacement is permanent, knowing that though Babylon may be very wrong, God has failed and we are helpless. This is the temptation for those of us who know better than to assimilate, but for whom resistance is a defensive posture without buoyancy or expectation. This response to displacement has most in common with the grim resolve of Stoicism.

3. The third possible response to exile, for persons who refuse assimilation and eschew despair, is to respond with *fresh, imaginative theological work*, recovering the old theological traditions and recasting them in terms appropriate to the new situation of faith in an alien culture. It is thus my urging that this new time of beginning for the church be a time and place for imaginative theological recasting that takes full account of the church's new cultural situation. This taking into account signifies that we are no longer chaplains for national legitimacy. For Americans generally and for white males in particular, it means that the story of Western domination and hegemony has come to an end.

Two things seem peculiarly important in understanding the analogy to exile. First, the new, imaginative activity now required does not scuttle the tra-

dition but stays very close to it; the activity does not seek a new rhetoric composed of new thought forms, but pays attention to what is given in the normative literature. Second, the new imaginative enterprise stays very, very
close to the present reality of suffering and displacement, and it insists that it
is precisely among those sufferings that fresh ways of faith will be given.

The response of exile upon which I shall focus by way of suggesting a
model is the poetry of Isaiah 40—55. There are other biblical materials that
could also be pursued, perhaps especially Job; for now, however, we will
consider Isaiah.

I make two preliminary observations about this poetry. First, it is deeply
grounded in tradition, enormously imaginative in articulation, and a hard,
disciplined, intellectual act of faith. Exilic reconstruction will require hard
intellectual work that makes linkages between past and present never before seen, and that risks utterances never before heard. Clearly this daring
intellectual activity not only shatters the old certitudes, but also renders
obsolete most of the old ideologies and all of our old, precious quarrels.

Second, for all the impressiveness of traditioning and imagination, the
core reality of this poetry as response to exile is its focal evangelical conviction. There is indeed a gospel of the nearness of God's governance.
Everything else flows from the conviction that God is working a newness,
has turned loose energy and power and promises amidst the realities of
contemporary public life. This daring liturgical, rhetorical claim, voiced in
passion and poetry, repositions Israel in exile, reshapes world history,
rereads Israel's destiny, and makes a promise that comes as demand. After
the sequence of God's *sovereign promise*, God's *sovereign demand*, and God's
sovereign absence that we have already considered, here is voiced God's *sovereign newness*.

Notice how the gospel is a precise antidote to the twin temptations of
exile. The sovereign newness of Yahweh refuses to despair that reality will
never change. The sovereign newness of Yahweh rejects the seduction of
Babylonian hegemony and the dominance of Babylonian gods. It is world
shattering and faith summoning to say as does the poet:

> Get you up to a high mountain,
>   O Zion, herald of good tidings;
> life up your voice with strength,
>   O Jerusalem, herald of good things,
>   lift it up, fear not;
> say to the cities of Judah,
>   "Behold your God!"
>
>   (Isa. 40:9)

> How beautiful upon the mountains
>   are the feet of him who brings good tidings,

> who publishes peace,
> who brings good tidings of good,
> who publishes salvation,
> who says to Zion, "Your God reigns."
>
> (Isa. 52:7)

There is offered in these announcements no explanation of how or why such a fresh, subversive, liberating word could be uttered. That word is uttered in the face of exile, the purpose of which is to silence all such speech and to stop all such utterance. What Israel knows in this moment of inversion, however, is that even imperial exile cannot stop sovereign newness from God. Israel's speech, no doubt enacted liturgically, no doubt on the lips of very human priests, no doubt deeply regretted by the imperial bureaucracy, was nonetheless uttered as God's own word and God's gift of newness.

Disciplines of Readiness

I imagine that like Israel, our American history has run its course in three moves from land yearning to land abusing to land losing, or conversely from sovereign promise to sovereign demand to sovereign absence. Now, in our wonderment, bafflement, and sometimes despair, we wonder if the plot has run out, or if like in our ancient paradigm, a new word can be uttered about God's stunning newness.

Of course we do not know if such a work can be spoken. We cannot coerce such a word from God, for the word is sovereign in freedom as in newness. Nor could we silence such a word if it were uttered. We can, however, at the sorry end of our present narrative, consider our readiness and prepare ourselves for the utterance of such a word. For that reason we need *disciplines of readiness*, acts to be undertaken with intentionality and discipline, to leave us ready if God should make new moves among us. This new readiness should permit a rethinking of what exiles must do that usually is not done by preexilic people. This new beginning is a new circumstance, not easily acknowledged by old-line and mainline faith, a circumstance that permits and requires fresh disciplines. From the assertion of the gospel in Isaiah 40—55, I suggest six such disciplines of readiness that are crucial for the receiving of God's newness and for converting exile into homecoming.

1. In the exile, Israel is driven back to its most *dangerous memories*. I suggest that in our exile, having played out our history of domination, we also are now driven back to our most elemental memories.

In Israel prior to exile there were two powerful temptations. On the one hand, Israel gave up remembering completely, scuttled the past and pretended that only the present had any pertinent claim upon the community.

Such a deep and systemic forgetting caused the present to be taken too seriously, to be valued too much, to be absolutized. On the other hand, Israel was tempted to substitute closer, more reasonable and respectable memories that were not so radical or so embarrassing. Israel could remember the founding of the holy temple and the royal monarchy and the possession of the land, but could not so well recall older memories of prerational needs, prerational gifts concerning the amazement of liberation, the miracle of manna, and the wonder of transformation.

The poet of the exile calls Israel back behind more convenient establishment memories to the definitional ones that lurk in Israel's past. The most elemental memory embraced by II Isaiah is the memory of Abraham and Sarah. The poet Second Isaiah explicitly enjoins Israel to return to that memory:

> Hearken to me, you who pursue deliverance,
>   you who seek the LORD.
> Look to the rock from which you were hewn,
>   and to the quarry from which you were digged.
> Look to Abraham your father,
>   and to Sarah who bore you;
> for when he was but one I called him,
>   and I blessed him and made him many.
>   (Isa. 51:1–2)

If you want to seek Yahweh, says the poet, seek Yahweh in the oldest, most embarrassing circumstance we ever had. Remember Abraham, who is on the one hand the strange, impressive father of faith who leaves at God's command, who goes into a new place, who carries blessing for others. But this same father in faith is on the other hand a pitiful figure of helplessness and fear, lying to save his skin, seeking a surrogate wife to get an heir, so unsure, so bewildered, so barely faithful.

When we have reflected long enough on Abraham, remember Sarah your mother. Sarah is the princess, the one after whom the great empire lusts, the mother of Isaac, the promise carrier. But remember more than that about her. Remember her oldness, her barrenness, her helplessness, her mocking laughter, her inability to receive the promised future. Remember her, because this pitiful old lady now laughs a new laugh, an Easter laugh, for God uses her very barrenness to create a newness. She is the model and anticipation of all barren mothers in our faith, of all barren people who have within them no gift of life and no capacity for faith. And yet God works a newness. God works a newness against all the evidence, in the face of deathly circumstance.

Remember Abraham and Sarah and then name all the names who worked "by faith."

> By faith Abraham obeyed. . . . By faith he sojourned in the land
> of promise. . . . By faith Sarah herself received power to conceive.
> . . . Therefore from one man, and him as good as dead, were born
> descendants as many as the stars of heaven. . . . These all died in
> faith, not having received what was promised but having seen it
> and greeted it from afar. (Heb. 11:8–13)

The whole tale is a tale "by faith."

Remember this cluster of dangerous memories, because this story models faith and invites to faith. Such remembering, embracing, recalling, celebrating, standing in solidarity with, is clearly a discipline of readiness. Isaiah 51 invites exiles to remember because they are short on faith, having nearly succumbed to the present imperial reality. In their doubt and despair they could not imagine a change in the present arrangements, and so they submitted and obeyed and resigned themselves. That would have been the end for them, except that the memory did its own powerful work in the community. The memory aroused faith in the power of God to work a newness.

The poet becomes lyrical about the impossible possibility:

> Fear not, for you will not be ashamed;
>   be not confounded, for you will not be put to shame;
> for you will forget the shame of your youth,
>   and the reproach of your widowhood you will remember no more.
> For your Maker is your husband,
>   the LORD of hosts is his name . . .
> For the LORD has called you
>   like a wife forsaken and grieved in spirit,
> like a wife of youth when she is cast off,
>   says your God.
>
>   (Isa. 54:4–6)

The shame of barrenness will be overcome. There will be compassion, overflowing love, and homecoming:

> For a brief moment I forsook you,
>   but with great compassion I will gather you.
> In overflowing wrath for a moment
>   I hid my face from you,
> but with everlasting love I will have compassion on you,
>   says the LORD, your Redeemer.
>   (Isa. 54:7–8)

Think what would happen to the energy and vitality of the church if we practiced the discipline of remembering. We are little inclined to perceive that our past has been lived "by faith." On the one hand we would rather proceed by "orthodoxy" or by "morality" than by the haunting requirement "by faith." On the other hand we would rather proceed on the basis of competence or by strategy. "By faith," however, cuts underneath our fearful morality and our ambitious strategies. "By faith" invites us to reperceive the world as a place where the power of God works when we can neither explain nor initiate.

The miracles remembered fit no ideology, but they create communities of possibility that the empire has been trying to prevent. People without memories settle for the way things now are. People in active touch with their memories become restless and filled with energy, prepared in a variety of ways to live beyond imperial definitions and boundaries. Exiles are the ones so needful that they risk newness outside royal rationality. Needy as they are, they are empowered from on high to act in freedom. The exiles are needful and empowered. This power, however, never visits us in our amnesia.

The old memories are not all contained in the ancient book. The history of the church is strewn with acts taken "by faith." What a service this new building would render if it were a place of sustained remembering, bearing daily and concrete testimony to the way in which God works life in the face of death, to the way in which God creates newness out of nothing, to the way in which hopeless faith discovers the power for life. The memory would not only permit but would insist on a very different present and on a future not domesticated. That is what happened for the listeners of the poem who went back into the memory they had neglected.

2. To be an exile and to resist assimilation and refuse despair, one must not grow too cozy with the host empire. It was a powerful temptation for exiled Jews, whose story had run out, to live themselves into the story of Babylon and to reidentify themselves as citizens of Babylon. Exiles in readiness, however, must practice critical distance from their context, indeed, must practice *dangerous criticism* to keep visible the destructive seduction of the empire that is too often covered over by euphemism. That criticism must assert both that the empire is incongruous with Yahweh's governance and that the empire cannot keep its promise of life.

The dangerous criticism voiced in the poetry of II Isaiah concerns two dimensions of the empire which are related but distinct. First, there is a *religious critique* of the empire. Every concentration of power needs its gods to bless it, to give credibility and legitimacy, to evoke loyalty and confidence. Every empire has such legitimating gods, however hidden they may be. But, says the poet, these gods are in fact a joke, because they have no power and they cannot save. The poet mocks them and invites his comrades to dismiss them:

Bel bows down, Nebo stoops,
　　their idols are on beasts and cattle;
these things you carry are loaded
　　as burdens on weary beasts.
They stoop, they bow down together,
　　they cannot save the burden,
but themselves go into captivity.
　　　　　　　　　　(Isa. 46:1–2)

The poet describes the ludicrous process by which gods have been man-
ufactured. They are created, not creators; they are objects, not subjects.
They are not self-starters, cannot take initiative, cannot work newness,
cannot give life.

Those who lavish gold from the purse,
　　and weigh out silver in the scales,
hire a goldsmith, and he makes it into a god;
　　then they fall down and worship!
They lift it upon their shoulders, they carry it,
　　they set it in its place, and it stands there;
　　it cannot move from its place.
If one cries to it, it does not answer
　　or save him from his trouble.
　　　　　　　　　　　　(Isa. 46:6–7)

These gods do not warrant allegiance and loyalty because they are mute
and passive; and if the gods of the empire are so helpless, so in the end is
the empire helpless. Though couched in clever poetry, this is a devastating
critique that declares the empire illegitimate. Its claims to legitimacy are a
hollow joke that the exiles boldly dismiss.

That critique of lack of legitimacy is made even more stark and daring
by the offer of an ultimate legitimacy for an alternative life. It is Yahweh,
not the imperial gods, who has power for life and who keeps promises. The
polemic against the other gods is resolved into doxology:

Hearken to me, O house of Jacob,
　　all the remnant of the house of Israel,
who have been borne by me from your birth,
　　carried from the womb;
even to your old age I am He,
　　and to gray hairs I will carry you,
I have made, and I will bear;
　　I will carry and will save.
　　　　　　　　　　　　(Isa. 46:3–4)

This God can act, has acted, and is now active. This one who acts can be trusted; the ones who cannot act deserve no loyalty or attention.

The religious critique is reenforced by a second critique of a very different kind. Chapter 47 continues to use theological rhetoric, but it in fact voices a *political critique* against entrenched power. The poem begins by anticipating the collapse and shame of the empire soon to be dismantled and humiliated. The empire had received all its greatness from Yahweh but had promptly violated Yahweh's mandate by showing no mercy (47:6). The poet makes the remarkable assertion that the condition for the durability of the empire is mercy to the exiles. The empire would not endure because of might and power or even because of wisdom but only because of policies of mercy. The problem with the empire is that it did not know that it had to answer to the merciful purpose of Yahweh. It imagined that it was autonomous and could do what it wanted to do. The empire repeatedly asserts its cynical notion of autonomy:

> You said, "I shall be mistress forever . . .
> I am, and there is no one besides me;
> I shall not sit as a widow
>   or know the loss of children . . .
> No one sees me . . .
> I am, and there is no one besides me."
>   (Isa. 47:7, 8, 10)

The exiles, however, know that cynical, autonomous power, no matter how massive and impressive it is, finally cannot have its way in the world. Inevitably, says the poet, a harsh end must come to such pretension.

> Behold, they are like stubble,
>   the fire consumes them;
> they cannot deliver themselves
>   from the power of the flame.
>   (Isa. 47:14)

The two critiques of religious legitimacy (in chapter 46) and of political autonomy (in chapter 47) together assert that the empire is precarious and tenuous and cannot sustain itself. I do not imagine that this heavy critique is in fact addressed directly to the Babylonians. Certainly the Babylonians would never have noticed or heeded such words. Rather the poetry is for the benefit of Israel's "overhearing." The overhearing is for the sake of the exiles themselves. They are being warned of complicity with the empire and invited to an alternative. The exiles, even at the failed end of their old narrative, know and trust enough to avoid such phony legitimacy and such seductive autonomy. The exiles are to have no part in such legitimacy and autonomy, and are to embrace an alternative that is neither phony nor seductive.

To be sure, the exiles had to work and shop daily in the empire. This literature, however, aims underneath such necessary involvements. It addresses Israel's imagination. It wants Israel's sensitivity weaned from imperial realities. It asserts that Israel is shaped and summoned for a more excellent way. But that more excellent way is not persuasive unless there is criticism that cuts through the imperial ideology and exposes the true character of the empire. In that time when Babylon seemed so awesome and in our time when dominant cultural values seem so irresistible, criticism of a daring kind is an act of readiness for homecoming. The prospect of being "born again" in exile is to be born to a new identity outside the empire. The exilic community must work at a critique that is not sectarian, not excessively partisan or elitist, but that names things by their right names. The truth is that the host empire is bent on earth and its gods cannot give life.

3. Assimilated exiles who accept the claims of the empire come to regard the empire as a final home where they shall always be. The power, threats, and gifts of the empire seem massive and absolute, ordained to perpetuity. When the claims and power of the empire are taken so seriously and are respected so deeply, the exilic community is incapable of thinking beyond the empire or of imagining a coming time when things will be greatly different. The empire has the strident capacity to domesticate exilic imagination and to co-opt Israel's capacity for hope. When hope is preempted by the empire, exiles cease to think about going home, abandon their precious notion of home, and settle for the empire as home. Such people cease to be exiles and redefine themselves as "at home" in the empire. The loss of home is then forfeiture of an intentional exilic status and of a hope beyond empire.

In order to resist such debilitating hopelessness, the exiles are invited to practice *dangerous promises*. The promises are centered around the sovereign faithfulness and the faithful sovereignty of Yahweh who will do what Yahweh says. This Yahwistic conviction is rooted in the memories of past promises that were kept. Reference to Yahweh and references to the past, however, are made in the service of a different future, a future fresh and new and joyous, not derived from what is, not extrapolated from the present, not the next stage in some development, but gift, intrusive surprise. The poet would have the exiles practice and maintain defiant speech that the empire will judge to be either silly or irrational. It is speech that asserts, posits, and envisions something not yet in hand, a gift to be given outside the empire, a gift the empire could never give and the empire could never deny.

The question posed for the exiles by the poet is this: What gifts are yet to be given that lie outside the control and competence of the empire? The empire characteristically insists that it is the single, all-sufficient source of gifts. The poet counters the empire by sounding another voice of promise:

Sing, O barren one, who did not bear;
    break forth into singing and cry aloud,
    you who have not been in travail!
For the children of the desolate one will be more
    than the children of her that is married, says the LORD.
Enlarge the place of your tent,
    and let the curtains of your habitations be stretched out;
hold not back, lengthen your cords and strengthen your stakes.
For you will spread abroad to the right and to the left,
    and your descendants will possess the nations
    and will people the desolate cities.

(Isa. 54:1–3)

The roles in this poem are easily assigned by the listening exiles. The "married one" who has children is Hagar, and the barren one is mother Sarah. The poem builds on an oxymoron, "barren mother." The poem is an assertion that eventually Sarah will bear more children than Hagar, though we know not how. Such a poem is remote from the exiles, of course, for in the sixth century they hardly cared about ancient Hagar and Sarah. Because of this remoteness, the poem must be reheard, listened to more carefully. A more intense listening yields a second scenario. The married one is Babylon. She is the one who is socially superior, seemingly approved in heaven and on earth, successful, secure, and self-satisfied. The barren one, mother Sarah, turns out to be the community of exiles, barren of heirs, bereft of historical possibility, abandoned, denied a future, without present joy or future prospects. The poet presents a terrible contrast between a shamed failure and a buoyant success, one humiliated, the other haughty. There seems to be no doubt about the locus of well-being for now and for all time to come.

The poem, however, assaults such a sure, obvious reading of reality. The poet counters the conventional assessments and speaks of an awesome inversion of historical reality. The barren one, Sarah, the old lady, the hopeless exile, is invited to sing, sing for joy, dance in amazement. The reason is that the children of this hopeless community will be more than the offspring of smug, hated Babylon. The future, says the poem, is more buoyant for the exiles than for the empire. The hopeless ones will swarm with children, be overwhelmed with newness, staggered by possibilities. The new life that is promised to this community of exiles will spread everywhere, beyond all limits and boundaries, rich with blessing.

The poem is candid. It acknowledges hopelessness, abandonment, and despair. It concedes that the present moment is a moment of God's angry abuse and painful silence. That, however, is only for a moment; then the *ḥesed* of God will be activated and life restored. God's fidelity endures and outflanks even the empire (Isa. 54:7–8). Life can begin again. The ones who were last will now be the first.

The important point is that the poem is outrageous and unreasonable. It invites exiles to sing against reality, to dance toward a future not even discernible, to praise the faithful God who will not be held captive by imperial reality. The singing and dancing and praising is an act of hope, a betting on God's capacity for an inexplicable future. It is the sort of hoping serious, baptized people must always do, always against the data, with trust in God's promise.

What is supposed to happen in this act of hope? Surely such a poem will not cause Babylon to retreat. Surely we know of no magic that will stagger the empire. The hoping of the poet has, however, another intent. Its purpose is to destabilize the present. Its intent is to break open the present system of domination for the sake of a new human possibility. Its purpose is to counter despair and to remind the exiles that they are children of a different trust, a trust in God's sovereign future not governed by the empire.

Think on our situation, where the hoping is only the domesticated promises that the free market system offers to insiders. But that is not really promise, rather simply an advantage. The relentlessness of imperial rationality wears down the buoyancy of seduced insiders and intimidated outsiders. So who is left to hope? Only the baptized, only those who regularly enter a zone of alternative possibility that is not rooted in present technology, but in gifts yet to be given, in promises yet to become visible, in gifts and promises guaranteed by God. The promises refuse to succumb to the rulers of this age. The promises stake out a way to live apart from the rulers of this age.

4. The people with dangerous memories and dangerous hopes may enter the present moment, not as resigned people, but with a strange, odd stance toward the way things are organized. Such bearers of danger must regularly work and eat and sleep. But they also gather regularly and restlessly in the liturgy, in a safe space where the "mother tongue" of trust is spoken. The liturgy is always the same. The kids always wonder why we do it one more time. Nonetheless one senses in this gathering a readiness and an expectation. There is a roll of drums, a blast of trumpets, waiting for the choir. And then they sing. They sing and people stand, stretching their necks to see. It is all choreographed, and yet there is an excitement about the music. There is a smattering of applause. Then the bold ones dance. The meeting is moved into awe and amazement and gratitude.

What has happened is that a *dangerous new song is being sung*. Exiles take music seriously and they sing dangerously. They sing what cannot be printed or announced officially:

> Sing to the LORD a new song,
> > his praise from the end of the earth!
> Let the sea roar and all that fills it,
> > the coastlands and their inhabitants.
> Let the desert and its cities lift up their voice,
> > the villages that Kedar inhabits;
> let the inhabitants of Sela sing for joy,
> > let them shout from the tops of the mountains.
> Let them give glory to the LORD,
> > and declare his praise in the coastlands.
> > > (Isa. 42:10–12)

Everyone sings. It is a new song, commissioned just for this meeting, never heard until now, and it grabs Israel in exile. It grabs all of creation. Everybody joins the song: the sea, the coastland, the desert, the cities, the villages. They all sing a new reality.

This is what they sing about: Yahweh is on the move! Yahweh has long been silent and is now active. Yahweh has been absent and is now powerfully present:

> The LORD goes forth like a mighty man,
> > like a man of war he stirs up his fury;
> he cries out, he shouts aloud,
> > he shows himself mighty against his foes.
> > > (Isa. 42:13)

Yahweh comes like a dangerous warrior and everyone yields before him. Yahweh comes as well like a mother in labor:

> For a long time I have held my peace,
> > I have kept still and restrained myself;
> now I will cry out like a woman in travail,
> > I will gasp and pant.
> > > (Isa. 42:14)

Yahweh comes and everything is changed:

> I will lay waste mountains and hills,
> > and dry up all their herbage;
> I will turn the rivers into islands,
> > and dry up the pools.
> And I will lead the blind
> > in a way that they know not,
> in paths that they have not known
> > I will guide them.
> I will turn the darkness before them into light,

the rough places into level ground.
These are the things I will do,
and I will not forsake them.
(Isa. 42:15–16)

The song is a song that names the name of Yahweh. Precious name! The naming of the name in the new song is a polemic. For every time the name is sung, some other pretender is dismissed. The affirmation of Yahweh always contains a polemic against someone else. Thus in its song, Israel might say:

Yahweh and not Baal.
Yahweh and not Dagon.
Yahweh and not Marduk.
Yahweh and not Zeus.
Yahweh and not Hobbes, not Adam Smith, not George Gilder.
Yahweh and not any pseudo-power.

Israel can sing like this because it knows that neither death nor life, nor angels nor principalities nor things present nor things to come can have their way with God's people in their singing and in their homecoming. The song dares to say in the most-vexed situations, "only Yahweh—none of the above."

The community of exiles sings new songs. If we listen to the singing, however, we discover that the new song is constituted by the same old words. The old words are recovered and reclaimed. Every song of exiles is a new singing of homecoming and possibility. The barren ones sing about the promised future. It may be that they will sing such innocuous-sounding phrases as "Glory to God in the highest," or "Praise God from whom all blessings flow." Even those familiar phrases are polemical, however, and stake out new territory for the God now about to be aroused to new caring. The songs of the church in exiled America have grown timid and feeble. In the face of such timidity and feebleness, we have these models of songs of transformation and healing, forgiveness and emancipation and resurrection; we have songs of Easter that assert the newness of Jesus in the face of death, songs of Christmas that assert the new messiah in the midst of a cosmic chaos, songs that devastate and energize, songs that dispatch to nullity and that evoke to possibility.

So what song did they sing in that old exile?

Yahweh has triumphed gloriously, the horse and the rider he
has thrown into the sea.
Yahweh has just become king.
Christ is risen, risen indeed.
Christ is born in a village, among the peasants.

You will notice that I am simply quoting the old formulations. Yet we call that "new, new song." How odd, that the new, new song is made up of the old, old story. The new doxology consists in the old songs we trusted before we succumbed, the lines we knew before we were embarrassed, the ones we prized before we capitulated to patriotic slogans and television jingles, the ones we trusted before we gave in to the dominant culture and its killing ideology.

The exiles are called to sing songs in a strange land; they discover in their singing that the land is not so strange. Even this alien land is claimed for the rule of Yahweh. We imagine in our modernity that singing is only cathartic or escapist, but that only shows our domestication. We need to remember how new songs have issued in new reality, remembering, for instance,

> That the civil rights movement was born on the singing lips of
> the suffering.
> That in South Africa, two Christmases ago, carols were banned
> because they evoked revolutionary energy and danger.

There is a lot to be said for the threat of such daring music; there is even more to be said for unruly, unruled imagination that dares to sing what is prohibited and outrageous and subversive, for such singing enthrones and dethrones, and the restless exiles sing until homecoming. In our exile, we will do well to study our failed singing and notice our fatigue and then notice how in our old songs, the invitations and possibilities are all there for those with freed lips and unadministered tongues. We may indeed yearn for a thousand tongues unfettered, tongues as the first member of our body to depart for home, all in singing.

5. As the poet moves toward the completion of Isaiah 40—55, a radical dimension is voiced that at first seems incidental. Exiles eat *dangerous bread*:

> Ho, every one who thirsts, come to the waters;
> and he who has no money, come, buy and eat!
> Come, buy wine and milk without money and without price.
> Why do you spend your money for that which is not bread,
>   and your labor for that which does not satisfy?
> Hearken diligently to me, and eat what is good,
>   and delight yourselves in fatness.
> Incline your ear, and come to me;
>   hear, that your soul may live.
>
> (Isa. 55:1–3)

This image and invitation are very different from all the others I have mentioned, less obviously a historical-theological category, more concrete and related to daily experience. It is in this image that the poet articulates the deep materiality of our faith, a materiality that begins in the valuing of creation and culminates in the incarnation, a materiality that knows all along that our bodies count decisively. What happens to our bodies? On the one hand they take in food. We must eat. On the other hand the food that is eaten is transformed into loyalty, energy, work, and care. The one who provides the food we eat governs the loyalties we embrace. The one who supplies our sustenance has claim upon the loyalty of the community. So we must pay attention to what we eat and to who feeds us.

This poem looks back to the startling wonder of alternative bread in the manna story of Exodus 16. The Israelites had lived long at the fleshpots of Egypt, and in their eating from the imperial hand had become slaves. Then they departed. As soon as they departed, hunger hit. Some wished to re-submit to the empire, embracing the bread of affliction and humiliation as the best way to avoid starvation. At the last moment, however, another bread is given. It is oddly given from heaven, from a source well beyond the plan of imperial bakers and brokers. The testimony of the narrative is that there is alternative bread and that we do not need to resubmit to Pharaoh in order to have food. This memory is on the horizon of the ex-ilic poet of Isaiah 55.

The same poem also looks forward, all the way to the stunning nar-rative of Daniel 1. Again the plot concerns the empire that always seems to control the bread. This time it is Nebuchadnezzar and the Babyloni-ans, the same ones who manage the exile in the time of II Isaiah. The imperial government, so the Daniel narrative states, seeks to recruit young men for government service. When the recruits arrive at the training table, Daniel and his profoundly vigilant colleagues refuse the rich imperial food. They opt for a diet of vegetables, which is a diet of faithfulness. When basic training is completed, Daniel and his friends are found to be "ten times better" than the ones who ate the rich seduc-tive food of Babylon. That the narrative has such an outcome should not surprise us. The poet in Isaiah 55 already knows that much about food. He knows that freedom, well-being, and power to act depend on an alternative bread that is provided neither by Egypt nor by Babylon. The old narrative and the later narrative sandwich our poem. All three texts assert that in order to have freedom to act, one must practice discrimi-nation with one's food.

The poem issues a profound invitation: come, buy, eat without money, without price. This is free food, food not given in order to coerce or se-duce or ingratiate. There is a free lunch. The food is free. The poem of in-vitation is at the same time a strong polemic. Why do you labor for that which does not satisfy? Why do you endlessly and passionately pursue such food that cannot keep its promise, so that after the meal is over you remain unfed, unnourished, uncared for? That bread is empty and lacks nourishing power. It is junk food. The poem is invitation, polemic, and in the end, it is promise. There will be delight in God's loyalty, which has been offered since the time of David, for now the same steadfast, sure loyalty is offered the exiles.

The poet with manna memories and Daniel hopes invites exilic Israel to cease taking life and food and nourishment and hope from the empire. The invitation is to desist from its hope, to disengage from its feast, to quit measuring loyalty by its claims. Of course the exiles will not disengage from this bread of the empire unless there is another bread available. What is offered is dangerous alternative bread; it is the very bread of the gospel, given outside the food supply of the empire.

What if Christians began to notice that certain kinds of bread enslave and are the bread of affliction? The most elemental faith decision we make concerns who feeds the body, and if the truth be told we are in various ways into "eating disorders" of a theological kind. We must reflect on bread and alternative bread. We may begin our reflections with Eucharist, the relentless enactment of our conviction that only broken bread feeds, only poured out wine contains the power of new life. But we daily resist the brokenness and refuse the poured-out-ness. We have become victims of junk food, the junk of social ideology, the attractiveness of consumerism, the killing seductions of security and despair; we are domesticated, silenced in our satiation. We scarcely notice that all these ersatz bakers have made promises they cannot keep.

What freedom there would be for us exiles if we left off the dominant hopes of our society, if we refused the dominant fears all around us, if we ate bread that hopes only evangelical possibility and that fears only the truth of God's faithfulness, utterly free of every other hope and every other fear! The problem, of course, is that we mostly eat imperial bread and do not notice its costs, that we wind up belonging and being owned, denied freedom for obedience. There will not be genuine freedom until, having new bread, we refuse the offer of Pharaoh's tasty bread. The new bread is, however, happening among us. We are seeing that we have neglected gospel bread and opted for imperial bread; we are left with the deep eating disorder of isolation, despair, and anxiety. The Eucharist is dangerous bread, as that dramatic act mediates to us a fresh way in the world now under the rule of God.

How odd that Jesus, after the feeding, meets the disciples at the sea. They are in a storm. Jesus speaks and the storm stops. The disciples are utterly astonished. At the end of the narrative, Mark adds tersely, perhaps enigmatically, "They did not understand about the loaves, but their hearts were hardened" (Mark 6:52). Hardness of heart consists, perhaps, in the notion that we already know and control all possible forms of bread. For control of bread eliminates the element of gift. The misreading of bread leads to much other misreading of the gospel and of life. We need not, however, so misread. There is another option.

6. These several dangers are enacted by the poet in the liturgy. Worship is the first place for danger. Worship is the time and place where the community gathers together its odd vocation and its dangerous destiny. Worship is the place where the community imaginatively anticipates its peculiar life in the world and enacts its displacement and homelessness, its deep yearning, and finally its joyous arrival home. Such an imaginative enactment of not being home and having a vision of home is what happens in these dangers of precious roots, daring criticism, new songs, fresh promises, and alternative bread.

Eventually, however, this company of exiles must move outside the liturgy into the reality of public life, must face the reality of Babylon and the risk of not being Babylonian. Thus the poet must speak about *dangerous departure* from the empire:

> Depart, depart, go out thence!
>   Touch no unclean thing;
> go out from the midst of her, purify yourselves,
>   you who bear the vessels of the LORD.
> For you shall not go out in haste,
>   and you shall not go in flight,
> for the LORD will go before you,
>   and the God of Israel will be your rear guard.
>   (Isa. 52:11–12)

The Jews in exile must act out this alternative, which is to be at home in defiance of the empire. The poet recalls the old departure of the exodus and issues a double imperative to do the same thing again: "depart, depart." In its second departure from the power of empire, Israel's homecoming must be uncontaminated by "unclean things," by any of the attractions or payoffs of the empire. Israel is to act out its otherness and its distinctiveness, eschewing every cultural power and temptation.

This departure is for Israel like the one in the book of Exodus, but it is also very different. That first time, our mothers and fathers hurried, leaving in a panic. This time there need be no hurry, no haste, no fear or panic. Go out with determination, but go out like first-class passengers. Why the tranquillity about this departure that seems so dangerous? Because Yahweh will go before you, the God of Israel will be your rear guard. The border patrol and the imperial police cannot lay a hand on you, because you are surrounded by this awesome bodyguard. Israel surrounded by Yahweh is utterly safe, protected, free from rush, on its way rejoicing. The last words of this extended poem are these:

> For you shall go out in joy,
>   and be led forth in peace;
> the mountains and the hills before you
>   shall break forth into singing,
>   and all the trees of the field shall clap their hands.
>
> (Isa. 55:12)

The departure is a great world event, and all the creatures take note of it. All the creatures rejoice in the homecoming because it is a sign that God is now powerfully at work to right the entire creation.

The departure envisioned by the poet is geographical, from the Euphrates to the Jordan. Long before the departure could be geographical, however, it had to be liturgical and imaginative, the community acting out in anticipation the daring break with all things imperial, thinking and envisioning itself free from all such support, stability, and reassurance. Out of the liturgical departure came ethical, political, and economic departure, Israel's choice to live life according to its call. Thus the second exodus is only incidentally geographical. The geographical reality followed readily from the more visceral disengagement and the embrace of an alternative vocation.

If I am correct that the mainline Christian tale has run out in exile, then I suggest that our sustained reflection on a dangerous departure is crucial work for us. We reflect upon a departure from the ideology of the empire, from militarism that produces fear, from consumerism that ends in satiated despair, from greed that breeds brutality, from ambition that ends in isolation, from competence that begets anxiety. We ponder a departure that enacts our baptismal freedom and identity. That departure, like its model in II Isaiah, likely has very little to do with geography. It is first and foremost a liturgical, imaginative departure that asserts our common baptism and then asserts a social-economic-political departure that liberates and sends us on our way rejoicing.

A Fresh Beginning

My suggestion is that our dominant tale has run out in exhaustion and displacement. In such a situation there is no easy or quick response. There is only the slow, hard work of poetic alternative. This poetic alternative begins in recognizing our true situation; it moves by subversive, evangelical lips uttering hopes and possibilities; it may end in new people, new community, new creation. The departure from the empire was the great point of risk for sixth-century Jews, but out of that departure came the birth of Judaism, the enactment of God's faithful capacity for newness.

This new beginning is only partly a looking back to end the war that has wrenched us so painfully apart. It is more an act of hope, a hunch that the narrative that has run out may be reentered in a fresh way. It is an act of hope that there might be birthed a new faith, a new mission, and a new worship that can again feed and nurture the body politic back to health.

Such newness is God's gift that God may give or withhold. We can only stand in readiness for what God may do. But that standing in readiness requires the use of intentional disciplines that in every case are marked by danger:

> *Dangerous memories* reaching all the way back to our barren mother Sarah.
> *Dangerous criticism* that mocks the deadly empire.
> *Dangerous promises* that imagine a shift of power in the world.
> *Dangerous songs* that sing of unexpected newness of life.
> *Dangerous bread* free of all imperial ovens; all leading to
> *Dangerous departures* of heart and body and mind, leavings undertaken in trust and obedience.

The gospel, in our moment of exhaustion, is a caring promise and a wondrous assertion that we belong and are intensely cared for:

> But now thus says the LORD,
>   he who created you, O Jacob,
>   he who formed you, O Israel:
> "Fear not, for I have redeemed you;
>   I have called you by name, you are mine.
> When you pass through the waters I will be with you;
>   and through the rivers, they shall not overwhelm you."
>   (Isa. 43:1–2)

The promise is given with marvelous evangelical poetic authority. We are now positioned to accept that promise and its traveling identity. Our reception of the promise is not a mission impossible. It is, however, an embrace of dangerous disciplines, whereby we wait for the wind, which may indeed come by here.

Abbreviations

AB	Anchor Bible
CBQ	*Catholic Biblical Quarterly*
GBS	*Guides to Biblical Scholarship*
HBT	*Horizons in Biblical Theology*
JBL	*Journal of Biblical Literature*
JSOT	*Journal for the Study of the Old Testament*
JSOTSup	Journal for the Study of the Old Testament—Supplement Series
OBT	Overtures to Biblical Theology
OTL	Old Testament Library
SBLSP	SBL Seminar Papers
SBT	Studies in Biblical Theology
SNTSMS	Society for New Testament Studies Monograph Series
SVTP	Studia in Veteris Testamenti pseudepigrapha
VTSup	Vetus Testamentum, Supplements
ZAW	*Zeitschrift für die alttestamentliche Wissenschaft*
ZTK	*Zeitschrift für Theologie und Kirche*

Notes

Chapter 1.
Preaching to Exiles

This chapter title is reminiscent of E. W. Nicholson, *Preaching to the Exiles: A Study of the Prose Tradition in the Book of Jeremiah* (Oxford: Basil Blackwell Publisher, 1970). Nicholson was one of the first in the recent discussion to discern the important role of exile in the generation of Old Testament faith. Nicholson in fact deals only with the late texts in the book of Jeremiah, which, in my discussion, I will not take up.

1. See Walter Brueggemann, "Disciplines of Readiness," chap. 8, and "Rethinking Church Models through Scripture," chap. 7, in this book.

2. Jack Stotts, "Beyond Beginnings," *Occasional Paper No. 2*, Theology and Worship Unit, Presbyterian Church (U.S.A.), 1992.

3. On the significance of metaphor for reading the biblical text and for theological reflections, see Phyllis Trible, *God and the Rhetoric of Sexuality* (OBT; Philadelphia: Fortress Press, 1978), 31–59, and Sallie McFague, *Metaphorical Theology: Models of God in Religious Language* (Philadelphia: Fortress Press, 1982), 1–66 and passim.

4. In my discussion of the church in relation to pluralism, I have decided not to address what I consider to be the related issue of the faltering of denominations. On that crisis, see Dorothy Bass, "Reflections on the Reports of Decline in Mainstream Protestantism," *Chicago Theological Seminary Register* 79 (1989): 5–15, and "Teaching with Authority? The Changing Place of Mainstream Protestantism in American Culture," *Religious Education* 85 (Spring 1990): 295–310.

5. On the trivializing of such symbols in the life of ancient Israel, see Peter Ackroyd, "The Temple Vessels: A Continuity Theme," VTSup 23 (1972): 166–81.

6. Jacob Neusner, *Understanding Seeking Faith: Essays on the Case of Judaism* (Atlanta: Scholars Press, 1986), 137–41, has shown how the historical-geographical experience of exile has become a paradigm for Judaism, so that Jews who did not share the actual concrete experience of exile must nonetheless appropriate

its paradigmatic power in order to be fully Jewish. In what follows, I am especially informed by the splendid study of Daniel L. Smith, *The Religion of the Landless: The Social Context of the Babylonian Exile* (Bloomington, Ind.: Meyer-Stone Books, 1989).

7. I use "world" here in the sense of Alfred Schutz, *Phenomenology of the Social World* (Evanston, Ill.: Northwestern University Press, 1967). A more accessible rendering of the same notion of world is found in Peter L. Berger and Thomas Luckmann, *The Social Construction of Reality: A Treatise in the Sociology of Knowledge* (Garden City, N.Y.: Doubleday & Co., 1966).

8. Stanley Hauerwas and William H. Willimon, *Resident Aliens: A Provocative Christian Assessment of Culture and Ministry for People Who Know That Something Is Wrong* (Nashville: Abingdon Press, 1989).

9. The long-term threat to the viability of faith is not right-wing religious, ominous and destructive as that is, but secularism. I think it most unfortunate that the church uses as much energy as it does on the former, when the latter is so pervasive and relentless among us.

10. On the theme of "political correctness," see Rosa Ehrenreich, "What Campus Radicals? The P.C. Undergrad Is a Useful Specter," *Harper's Magazine* (December 1991): 57–61; and Louis Menand, "What Are Universities For? The Real Crisis on Campus Is One of Identity," *Harper's Magazine* (December 1991): 47–56.

11. Martin Buber, *Between Man and Man* (New York: Macmillan Co., 1965), 126, writes: "In the history of the human spirit, I distinguish between epochs of habitation and epochs of homelessness." Buber understands our own epoch to be one of homelessness. On the same theme, informed by Buber, see Nicholas Lash, "Eclipse of Word and Presence," *Easter in Ordinary: Reflections on Human Experience and the Knowledge of God* (Charlottesville, Va.: University Press of Virginia, 1988), 199–218.

12. The disregard of "late Judaism" in Christian scholarship and theological education reflects the power of the "Wellhausian hypothesis" in which the postexilic period was regarded as degenerate, inferior, and not worthy of attention. More recent scholarship has to some modest extent broken loose of the grip of that hypothesis in order that the period can be taken with theological seriousness.

13. Peter Ackroyd, *Exile and Restoration: A Study of Hebrew Thought of the Sixth Century B.C.* (OTL; Philadelphia: Westminster Press, 1968).

14. Ralph W. Klein, *Israel in Exile: A Theological Interpretation* (OBT; Philadelphia: Fortress Press, 1979).

15. Smith, *Religion of the Landless*. Smith's study represents a most important advance beyond Ackroyd and Klein in terms of method, as he pays attention to the interaction between the social realities of the exile and its impact upon the way in which literature functions.

16. It is evident that I will proceed with something like a "method of correlation" not unlike that proposed by Paul Tillich. I find such an approach practically useful in establishing a "dynamic analogy" with the text for our own time. The method is a convenience for me and reflects no commitment to a program like that of Tillich, about which I have great reservations.

17. See Delbert R. Hillers, *Lamentations: A New Translation with Introduction and Commentary* (AB 7A; Garden City, N.Y.: Doubleday & Co., 1972), xl–xli.

18. For a critical understanding of the function of the genealogies, see Marshall D. Johnson, *The Purpose of the Biblical Genealogies: With Special Reference to the Genealogies of Jesus* (SNTSMS 8; London: Cambridge University Press, 1969), and Robert R. Wilson, *Genealogy and History in the Biblical World* (New Haven, Conn.: Yale University Press, 1977).

19. A wonderful example of such stories and such characters to people's imagination are the biographical statements by Russell Baker, *Growing Up* (New York: New American Library-Dutton, 1983) and *The Good Times* (New York: New American Library-Dutton, 1991).

20. Cf. Ex. 32:32f.; Isa. 4:3; 56:5; Dan. 12:1; Rev. 3:5; 13:8; 17:8; 20:12, 15; 21:27.

21. Rolf Rendtorff, "Die theologische Stellung des Schöpfungsglaubens bei Deuterojesaja," *ZTK* (1954): 3–13; Rainer Albertz, *Weltschöpfung und Menschenschöpfung: Untersucht bei Deuterojesaja, Hiob und in den Psalmen* (Calwer Theologische Monographien 3; Stuttgart: Calwer Verlag, 1974).

22. On "as" as "the copula of imagination," see Garrett Green, *Imagining God: Theology and the Religious Imagination* (New York: Harper & Row, 1989), 73, 140, and passim.

23. Ackroyd, "The Temple Vessels: A Continuity Theme," shows how the temple vessels can be narrated to report a complete and decisive break in historical continuity, or conversely, can be used to enact continuity in the midst of enormous discontinuity.

24. On the general theme and problem of presence, see Samuel Terrien, *The Elusive Presence: Toward a New Biblical Theology* (Religious Perspectives 26; New York: Harper & Row, 1978). More specifically on presence as understood in the Priestly tradition, see Robert B. Coote and David Robert Ord, *In the Beginning: Creation and the Priestly History* (Minneapolis: Fortress Press, 1991), especially chapters 9–11.

25. Paul Ricoeur, *The Symbolism of Evil* (Boston: Beacon Press, 1967), 255–60, traces the way in which Genesis portrays human persons as both *perpetrators* and *victims*. Already in that narrative, which is characteristically read as though it concerned only fault, Israel has carefully nuanced the ambiguity in social experience.

26. See Samuel Terrien, "Job as a Sage," in *The Sage in Israel and the Ancient Near East*, ed. John G. Gammie and Leo G. Perdue (Winona Lake, Ind.: Eisenbrauns, 1990), 231–42, and Rainer Albertz, "The Sage Adds Pious Wisdom in the Book of Job: The Friends' Perspective," ibid., 243–61.

27. Concerning these narratives, I am primarily informed by Smith, *Religion of the Landless*, 153–78.

28. Green, *Imagining God*, 41–60, has taught me the most concerning the fact that our "givens" are dependent upon paradigmatic construals of reality. On the cruciality of rhetoric for reality, see the suggestive interface of religion and rhetoric suggested by Wayne C. Booth, "Rhetoric and Religion: Are They Essentially Wedded?" in *Radical Pluralism and Truth: David Tracy and the Hermeneutics of Religion*, ed. Werner G. Jeanrond and Jennifer L. Rike (New York: Crossroad, 1991), 62–80.

29. On the use of the notion of liminality from Victor Turner in the interest of religious transformation, see Urban T. Holmes, "The Priest as Enchanter," in *To Be a Priest: Perspectives on Vocation and Ordination*, ed. Robert E. Terwilliger and Urban T. Holmes (New York: Harper & Row, 1975), 173–81, and Marchita B. Mauck, "The Liminal Space of Ritual and Art," in *The Bent World: Essays on Religion and Culture*, ed. John R. May (Chico, Calif.: Scholars Press, 1981), 149–57.

30. See Roy Schafer, *Retelling a Life: Narration and Dialogue in Psychoanalysis* (New York: Basic Books, 1992), especially chapter 2.

31. See William H. Willimon, *Peculiar Speech: Preaching to the Baptized* (Grand Rapids: Wm. B. Eerdmans Publishing Co., 1992).

32. The critique often leveled against Willimon and Hauerwas, that they are sectarian, is driven by the long-established categories of H. Richard Niebuhr concerning "Christ and Culture." It is now clear that those older categories are no longer adequate for the actual situation of the church in Western culture and that a critique must be made of Niebuhr's typology. See, for example, Robert E. Webber, *The Church in the World: Opposition, Tension, or Transformation?* (Grand Rapids: Zondervan Publishing House, 1986), 261–78 and passim.

33. Smith, *Religion of the Landless*, 127–38, provides a most discerning study of the letter concerning the "social psychology of a group under stress."

34. Karl Barth, *Church Dogmatics* IV/1 (Edinburgh: T. & T. Clark, 1956) #59, 157–210.

35. Ibid., 180–83, 188–94.

36. Karl Barth, *Church Dogmatics* IV/2 (Edinburgh: T. & T. Clark, 1958) #64, 20–154. On the parable of Luke 15:11–32, see pp. 21–25.

37. On the "impossibilities" of the kingdom, see Walter Brueggemann, "'Impossibility' and Epistemology in the Faith Traditions of Abraham and Sarah (Genesis 18:1–15)," *ZAW* (1982): 615–34.

Chapter 2.
Cadences That Redescribe: Speech among Exiles

1. On my understanding of exile as a useful metaphor for the contemporary crisis of the U.S. church, see Walter Brueggemann, "Disciplines of Readiness," chap. 8, and "Preaching to Exiles," chap. 1, in this book.

2. Alan Mintz, *Ḥurban: Responses to Catastrophe in Hebrew Literature* (New York: Columbia University Press, 1984), x. I am indebted to Tod Linafelt for this most remarkable reference.

3. Mintz, *Ḥurban*, 2. I have added the italics.

4. Paul Ricoeur, "Biblical Hermeneutics," *Semeia* 4 (1975): 107–45.

5. The "odd speech" with which Ricoeur deals includes proclamatory sayings, proverbs, and parables. Compare "Biblical Hermeneutics," 109–18.

6. Ricoeur, "Biblical Hermeneutics," 31, 127, and passim.

7. The basic book on lamentation is Claus Westermann, *Praise and Lament in the Psalms* (Atlanta: John Knox Press, 1981).

8. Mintz, *Ḥurban*, 17–48, has the most suggestive discussion of the book of

Lamentations known to me. The most reliable commentary is Delbert R. Hillers, *Lamentations: A New Translation with Introduction and Commentary* (AB 7A; Garden City, N.Y.: Doubleday & Co., 1972).

9. Mintz, *Ḥurban*, 24, most helpfully discerns what is at stake in this particular imagery:

> The serviceableness of the image of Jerusalem as an abandoned fallen woman lies in the precise register of pain it articulates. An image of death would have purveyed the false comfort of finality; the dead have finished with suffering and their agony can be evoked only in retrospect. The raped and defiled woman who survives, on the other hand, is a living witness to a pain that knows no release. It is similarly the perpetualness of her situation that comes through most forcefully when Zion is pictured as a woman crying bitterly alone in the night with tears wetting her face (1:2). The cry seems to ululate permanently in the night; the tear forever falls to the cheek. It is a matter not just of lingering suffering but of continuing exposure to victimization.

10. The contrast between the book of Lamentations and Psalm 74 is the difference between "lament" and "complaint." Erhard Gerstenberger, "Jeremiah's Complaints: Observations on Jer. 15:10–21," *JBL* 82 (1963): 405, n. 50, draws the distinction nicely: "A lament bemoans a tragedy which cannot be reversed, while a complaint entreats God for help in the midst of tribulation." The distinction and interrelatedness of the two are nicely expressed in German: *Klage* and *Anklage*.

11. On the cruciality of coming to speech, see Elaine Scarry, *The Body in Pain: The Making and Unmaking of the World* (New York: Oxford University Press, 1985), and Judith Lewis Herman, *Trauma and Recovery: The Aftermath of Violence—From Domestic Abuse to Political Terror* (New York: Basic Books, 1992).

12. There is a powerful play of imagery in the relation between Jerusalem as an abused widow and Yahweh as a restless woman about to give birth.

13. The most complete study of the genre is by Edgar W. Conrad, *Fear Not Warrior: A Study of 'al tira' Pericopes in the Hebrew Scriptures* (Brown Judaic Studies 75; Chico, Calif.: Scholars Press, 1985).

14. Joseph Sittler, *Grace and Gravity: Reflections and Provocations* (Minneapolis: Augsburg Publishing House, 1986), 99–100. See the more comprehensive discussion by Gail R. O'Day, "Toward a Biblical Theology of Preaching," in *Listening to the Word: Studies in Honor of Fred B. Craddock*, ed. Gail R. O'Day and Thomas G. Long (Nashville: Abingdon Press, 1993), 17–32.

15. Claus Westermann, "The Way of the Promise Through the Old Testament," in *The Old Testament and Christian Faith: A Theological Discussion*, ed. Bernhard W. Anderson (New York: Harper & Row, 1963), 202–9.

16. On this text, see Walter Brueggemann, "A Shattered Transcendence?: Exile and Restoration," in *Problems and Prospects in Biblical Theology*, ed. Steven J. Kraftchick et al. (Nashville: Abingdon Press, 1995), 169–82.

17. I name economics and sexuality, because these are the twin issues that vex and

will continue to vex the church. It will be helpful to see that the two are deeply interrelated, as the parallel criticisms of Marx and Freud make clear.

18. See Walter Brueggemann, "Praise and the Psalms: A Politics of Glad Abandonment," Part I, *The Hymn: A Journal of Congregational Song* 43(3) (July 1992), 14–19, Part II, ibid. 43(4) (October 1992): 14–18.

19. See the helpful discussion of this passage by Norbert Lohfink, *The Covenant Never Revoked: Biblical Reflections on Christian-Jewish Dialogue* (Mahwah, N.J.: Paulist Press, 1991), 45–57. Lohfink makes clear that the text cannot be interpreted in a Christian, supersessionist way.

20. On "forgiveness," see especially the exilic text of 1 Kings 8:27–53.

21. On the practice of promise among exiles in order to fight off despair, see Rubem A. Alves, *Tomorrow's Child: Imagination, Creativity, and the Rebirth of Culture* (New York: Harper & Row, 1972), 182–205. Alves writes, "Why is it so important to go on hoping? Because without hope one will be either dissolved in the existing state of things or devoured by insanity" (p. 193).

22. My use of the term "end" here as a sense of terrible loss is intended to counter the argument of Francis Fukuyama, *The End of History and the Last Man* (New York: Free Press, 1992). In my judgment his self-serving argument, that is, self-serving for Western capitalism, is a romantic fantasy. He understands the current "end" to be one of triumph.

23. Mintz, *Ḥurban*, 29.

Chapter 3.
Preaching as Reimagination

1. See Richard Rorty, *Philosophy and the Mirror of Nature* (Princeton, N.J.: Princeton University Press, 1979), 335 and passim.

2. I am aware that the term "handmaiden" is the employment of a term beset with a history of sexism. I use it here intentionally and in recognition of what it implies for historical criticism.

3. On the presuppositional, intellectual, and ideological revolution wrought in the rise of criticism, see Paul Hazard, *The European Mind: The Critical Years 1680–1715* (New York: Fordham University Press, 1990), and Susan Bordo, *The Flight to Objectivity: Essays on Cartesianism and Culture* (Albany, N.Y.: SUNY Press, 1987).

4. On what I call "the emerging criticisms," see Steven L. McKenzie and Stephen R. Haynes, eds., *To Each Its Own Meaning: An Introduction to Biblical Criticisms and Their Applications* (Louisville, Ky.: Westminster/John Knox Press, 1993).

5. I understand that it is conventional to view most worshiping congregations as profoundly homogeneous, and that is no doubt true. But within such homogeneous communities, it is increasingly the case that there are wide-ranging convictions and opinions, so wide-ranging that it is often difficult to identify any basis of consensus. Such heterogeneity is very different from a kind of diversity rooted in a shared core of perspective.

6. See David Lochhead, *The Dialogical Imperative: A Christian Reflection on Interfaith Encounter* (Maryknoll, N.Y.: Orbis Books, 1988), and especially David Tracy, *Plurality and Ambiguity: Hermeneutics, Religion, Hope* (New York: Harper & Row, 1987).

7. Alasdair MacIntyre, *Three Rival Versions of Moral Enquiry: Encyclopaedia, Genealogy, and Tradition* (Notre Dame, Ind.: University of Notre Dame Press, 1990), has observed that in even such a formidable situation as the Gifford Lectures, a changed epistemological climate now permits the lecturer only to make a proposal, but not to announce a conclusion to be received by the audience.

8. See the famous distinction made by Krister Stendahl, "Biblical Theology, Contemporary," in *The Interpreter's Dictionary of the Bible A–D* (Nashville: Abingdon Press, 1962), 418–32, and the critical response of Ben Ollenburger, "What Krister Stendahl 'Meant'—A Normative Critique of 'Descriptive Biblical Theology,'" *HBT* 8[1] (June 1986): 61–98.

9. See especially Susan A. Handelman, *The Slayers of Moses: The Emergence of Rabbinic Interpretation in Modern Literary Theory* (Albany, N.Y.: SUNY Press, 1982).

10. Ibid., 21, 34, and passim. See also Moshe Idel, "Infinities of Torah in Kabbalah," in *Midrash and Literature*, ed. Geoffrey H. Hartman and Sanford Budick (New Haven, Conn.: Yale University Press, 1986), 141–57, and more generally the entire volume.

11. See Handelman, *The Slayers of Moses*, 141–52 and passim.

12. Paul Ricoeur, "From the Hermeneutics of Texts to the Hermeneutics of Action," *From Text to Action: Essays in Hermeneutics II* (Evanston, Ill.: Northwestern University Press, 1991), 105–222. See also Richard Harvey Brown, *Society as Text: Essays on Rhetoric, Reason, and Reality* (Chicago: University of Chicago Press, 1987).

13. Ricoeur, *From Text to Action*, 121.

14. On the "classic," see David Tracy, *The Analogical Imagination: Christian Theology and the Culture of Pluralism* (New York: Crossroad, 1981).

15. See the discussion of Paul Ricoeur, "Biblical Hermeneutics," *Semeia* 4 (1975): 127 and passim. In a very different frame of reference, see also the notion of "construal" and reconstrual in David H. Kelsey, *The Uses of Scripture in Recent Theology* (Philadelphia: Fortress Press, 1975).

16. Philip Rieff, *The Triumph of the Therapeutic: Uses of Faith after Freud* (New York: Harper & Row, 1966). More generally on the Enlightenment, see Susan Bordo, *The Flight to Objectivity*, and Stephen Toulmin, *Cosmopolis: The Hidden Agenda of Modernity* (New York: Free Press, 1990). In *Texts Under Negotiation: The Bible and Postmodern Imagination* (Minneapolis: Fortress Press, 1993), chapter 1, I have tried to assess the significance of the changes in Enlightenment consciousness for biblical interpretation.

17. In addition to Paul Hazard, *The European Mind*, see Klaus Scholder, *The Birth of Modern Critical Theology: Origins and Problems of Biblical Criticism in the Seventeenth Century* (Philadelphia: Trinity Press International, 1990).

18. Bordo, *The Flight to Objectivity*, suggests that the loss of "mother church" required finding another certitude that could nurture like a mother.

19. On the emergence of the individual self in the Cartesian program, see Charles Taylor, *Sources of the Self: The Making of the Modern Identity* (Cambridge, Mass.: Harvard University Press, 1989).

20. For a positive alternative to such individualism, see Paul R. Sponheim, *Faith and the Other: A Relational Theology* (Minneapolis: Fortress Press, 1993).

21. See Milton L. Myers, *The Soul of Modern Economic Man* (Chicago: University of Chicago Press, 1983), on the "text" of Hobbes behind the work of Adam Smith.

22. See the work of Neil Postman, *Entertaining Ourselves to Death: Public Discourse in the Age of Show Business* (New York: Penguin Books, 1986), and *Technology: The Surrender of Culture to Technology* (New York: Random House, 1993).

23. See Godfrey Hodgson, *The Colonel: The Life and Wars of Henry Stimson 1867–1950* (New York: Alfred A. Knopf, 1990).

24. See Walter Isaacson and Evan Thomas, *Wise Men: Six Friends and the World They Made* (New York: Touchstone Books, 1988). Of the "Wise Men," Kai Bird, *The Chairman, John J. McCloy: The Making of the American Establishment* (New York: Simon & Schuster, 1992), 663, writes: "As men possessing a measure of *gravitas*, McCloy and other Establishment figures always claimed they could rise above the private interests they represented and discern the larger public good. Ultimately, this claim is not sustainable."

25. Adrian Desmond and James Moore, *Darwin* (New York: Warner Books, 1991), make a compelling case that "social Darwinism" was not remote from the awareness of Darwin himself. He knew where he was located socially as he did his research.

26. See the discussion of David McLellan, *The Thought of Karl Marx: An Introduction* (London: Macmillan & Co., 1971), 41–51.

27. Concerning the role of "social theatre" in the establishment and maintenance of social relations, see E. P. Thompson, *Customs in Common* (New York: New Press, 1991), 86–87 and passim.

28. See Leon Festinger, *A Theory of Cognitive Dissonance* (Palo Alto, Calif.: Stanford University Press, 1962).

29. Victor Turner, *The Ritual Process: Structure and Anti-Structure* (Ithaca, N.Y.: Cornell University Press, 1969). For an exposition and critique of Turner's work, see Bobby C. Alexander, *Victor Turner Revisited: Ritual as Social Change* (Atlanta: Scholars Press, 1991).

30. The basic study of this coherence is Robert Bellah, "Civil Religion in America," *Daedalus* 96 (winter 1967): 1–21. See his larger discussion in *The Broken Covenant: American Civil Religion in Time of Trial* (New York: Crossroad, 1975). Part of the power of Martin Luther King, Jr., is that he was still able to appeal to this coherence.

31. In *Texts Under Negotiation: The Bible and Postmodern Imagination* (Minneapolis: Augsburg Fortress, 1993), 2–25, I have suggested that the work of scripture interpretation is to "fund" counterimagination.

32. Wallace Stevens, "A High-Toned Old Christian Woman," in *The Collected Poems of Wallace Stevens* (New York: Vintage Books, 1954), 59.

33. Garrett Green, *Imagining God: Theology and the Religious Imagination* (San Francisco: Harper & Row, 1989), 73, 140, and passim.

34. David J. Bryant, *Faith and the Play of Imagination: On the Role of Imagination in Religion* (Macon, Ga.: Mercer University Press, 1989), 115, helpfully explores what it means to "take as."

35. On the "myth of the given," in addition to Thomas Kuhn, *The Structure of Scientific Revolutions* (Chicago: University of Chicago Press, 1976), see also the

important work of Mary Hesse and Michael Arbib, *The Construction of Reality* (Cambridge: Cambridge University Press, 1986).

36. The claim of David R. Blumenthal, *Facing the Abusing God: A Theology of Protest* (Louisville, Ky.: Westminster/John Knox, 1993), 47–54 and passim, that we live *ad seratim*, has much to commend it. But it is likely an overstatement for anyone.

37. See Brevard S. Childs's most recent statement in his *Biblical Theology of the Old and New Testaments: Theological Reflection on the Christian Bible* (Minneapolis: Fortress Press, 1992), 70–94 and passim.

38. Toulmin, *Cosmopolis*, 186–201, has nicely argued positively for a retreat from universal assertion.

39. See, for example, Gabriel Josipovici, *The Book of God: A Response to the Bible* (New Haven, Conn.: Yale University Press, 1988), 75–89, and his treatment of the Joseph narrative.

40. John R. Donahue, *The Gospel in Parable* (Philadelphia: Fortress Press, 1988), has provided a rich study of the parables and fully understands the parabolic character of gospel truth. He observes (212) the cruciality of such speech when living in a "desert of the imagination."

41. Sandra M. Schneiders, *The Revelatory Text: Interpreting the New Testament as Sacred Scripture* (San Francisco: Harper, 1991), 102–108.

42. According to Jacob Neusner (*The Enchantments of Judaism: Rites of Transformation from Birth through Death* [New York: Basic Books, 1987], 214), "We are Jews through the power of our imagination."

43. On the history of imagination, see Green, *Imagining God*, chapter 1, and Richard Kearney, *The Wake of Imagination* (Minneapolis: University of Minnesota Press, 1988) and *Poetics of Imagining: From Husserl to Lyotard* (San Francisco: Harper, 1991).

44. Kearney, *Poetics of Imagining*, 88–111, provides a useful entry to Bachelard. It is from Kearney that I have taken my lead here. Of the work of Bachelard, see *The Poetics of Space* (Boston: Beacon Press, 1969) and *On Poetic Imagination*, ed. Colette Gandin (New York: Bobbs-Merrill Co., 1971).

45. Kearney, *Poetics of Imagining*, 95.

46. John E. Thiel, *Imagination and Authority: Theological Authorship in the Modern Tradition* (Minneapolis: Fortress Press, 1991).

47. The statement is programmatic for Ricoeur. See, for example, Ricoeur, *The Conflict of Interpretations* (Evanston, Ill.: Northwestern University Press, 1974), 288.

48. On imagination as the originary point of possibility, see Paul Ricoeur, *The Philosophy of Paul Ricoeur*, ed. Charles E. Reagan and David Stewart (Boston: Beacon Press, 1978), 231–38.

49. Brueggemann, *Texts Under Negotiation*, 64–70.

50. Hans Urs von Balthasar, *Theo-Drama: Theological Dramatic Theory I, Prolegomena* (San Francisco: Ignatius Press, 1988), *Theo-Drama: Theological Dramatic Theory II, The Dramatis Personae: Man in God* (San Francisco: Ignatius Press, 1990); Frances Young, *Virtuoso Theology: The Bible and Interpretation* (Cleveland: Pilgrim Press, 1993).

51. G. Ernest Wright, *God Who Acts: Biblical Theology as Recital* (SBT 8; London:

SCM Press, 1952); G. Ernest Wright and Reginald H. Fuller, *The Book of the Acts of God: Christian Scholarship Interprets the Bible* (Garden City, N.Y.: Doubleday & Co., 1957); and C. H. Dodd, *The Apostolic Preaching and Its Developments* (New York: Harper & Brothers, n.d.).

52. See, for example, Owen C. Thomas, ed., *God's Activity in the World: The Contemporary Problem* (Chico, Calif.: Scholars Press, 1983); James B. Wiggins, ed., *Religion as Story* (New York: University Press of America, 1975); and Stanley Hauerwas and L. Gregory Jones, eds., *Why Narrative? Readings in Narrative Theology* (Grand Rapids: Wm. B. Eerdmans Publishing Co., 1989).

53. On dramatic rendering as it pertains to theological discourse, see Dale Patrick, *The Rendering of God in the Old Testament* (OBT; Philadelphia: Fortress Press, 1981).

54. Hayden White, "The Politics of Historical Interpretation: Discipline and De-Sublimation," in *The Politics of Interpretation*, ed. W.J.T. Mitchell (Chicago: University of Chicago Press, 1983), 119–43; *The Content of the Form: Narrative Discourse and Historical Representation* (Baltimore: Johns Hopkins University Press, 1987); and *Metahistory: The Historical Imagination in Nineteenth Century Europe* (Baltimore: Johns Hopkins University Press, 1973).

55. Alasdair MacIntyre, *Whose Justice? Which Rationality?* (Notre Dame, Ind.: University of Notre Dame Press, 1988).

56. Amos Wilder, "Story and Story-World," *Interpretation* 37 (1983): 353–64. See my summary on "world-making" in Walter Brueggemann, *The Praise of Israel: Doxology Against Idolatry and Ideology* (Philadelphia: Fortress Press, 1988), 1–28, 157–60.

57. Brevard S. Childs, "Psalm Titles and Midrashic Exegesis," *Journal of Semitic Studies* 16 (1971): 137–50.

58. On the cruciality of rhetoric, see the suggestive distinction made by Richard A. Lanham, *The Motives of Eloquence: Literary Rhetoric in the Renaissance* (New Haven, Conn.: Yale University Press, 1976), 1–35, between "rhetorical man" and "serious man." And see the comments upon Lanham's distinction by Stanley Fish, "Rhetoric," in *Critical Terms for Literary Study*, ed. Frank Lentricchia and Thomas McLaughlin (Chicago: University of Chicago Press, 1990), 206–9. Such arguments suggest that the privilege long assigned to Plato and Aristotle against the Sophists may be usefully reexamined.

59. See, for example, Numbers 11:4–6; 14:1–4; Exodus 16:3.

60. Brueggemann, *Texts Under Negotiation*, 21–25.

61. Walter Brueggemann, *Biblical Perspectives on Evangelism: Living in a Three-Storied Universe* (Nashville: Abingdon Press, 1993).

62. Peter L. Berger and Thomas Luckmann, *The Social Construction of Reality: A Treatise in the Sociology of Knowledge* (Garden City, N.Y.: Doubleday & Co., 1967), 156–57.

63. For a standard summary of critical judgments about Deuteronomy, see Patrick D. Miller, *Deuteronomy* (Interpretation; Louisville, Ky.: Westminster/John Knox Press, 1990), 2–17.

64. See Thompson, *Customs in Common*, as in n. 27, above.

65. See Walter Brueggemann, "As the Text 'Makes Sense': Keep the Methods as Lean and Uncomplicated as Possible," *Christian Ministry* 14 (November 1983): 7–10.

Chapter 4.
Testimony as a Decentered Mode of Preaching

1. See Klaus Scholder, *The Birth of Modern Critical Theology: Origins and Problems of Biblical Criticism in the Seventeenth Century* (Philadelphia: Trinity Press International 1990).

2. See Paul Hazard, *The European Mind: The Critical Years 1680–1715* (New York: Fordham University Press, 1990).

3. George A. Lindbeck, *The Nature of Doctrine: Religion and Theology in a Postliberal Age* (Philadelphia: Westminster Press, 1984), recognizes that propositional theology is one of the major distortions of proper theological interpretation, but he does not take it as the target of his major critique.

4. Stephen Toulmin, *Cosmopolis: The Hidden Agenda of Modernity* (New York: Free Press, 1990), has demonstrated the inclination of modernity toward universals. See especially pp. 30–35, 186–92.

5. For one review of the practical dimensions of the crisis, see Loren B. Mead, *The Once and Future Church: Reinventing the Congregation for a New Mission Frontier* (Washington, D.C.: Alban Institute, 1991).

6. Martin Luther, "The Babylonian Captivity of the Church," in *Three Treatises* (Philadelphia: Muhlenburg Press, 1960), 115–260.

7. See Walter Brueggemann, "Preaching to Exiles," chap. 1, and "Cadences That Redescribe: Speech among Exiles," chap. 2, in this book.

8. On language appropriate to the freedom and danger of God, see Stephen H. Webb, *Re-Figuring Theology: The Rhetoric of Karl Barth* (Albany, N.Y.: SUNY Press, 1991).

9. See the analysis of Paul Ricoeur, "The Hermeneutics of Testimony," in *Essays on Biblical Interpretation* (Philadelphia: Fortress Press, 1980), 119–54, on biblical genres of testimony.

10. This interpretive clue is proposed by Frank M. Cross. See the most recent discussion of the text by Paul D. Hanson, *Isaiah 40–66* (Interpretation; Louisville, Ky.: Westminster John Knox Press, 1995), 13–26.

11. On "strategies of saturation," see Walter Brueggemann, *Biblical Perspectives on Evangelism: Living in a Three-Storied Universe* (Nashville: Abingdon Press, 1993), 95–120.

12. This reading is in the LXX, on which see P. Kyle McCarter Jr., *I Samuel: A New Translation with Introduction and Commentary* (AB 8; Garden City, N.Y.: Doubleday & Co., 1980), 208–14.

13. On this phrasing, see Emil Fackenheim, *God's Presence in History: Jewish Affirmations and Philosophical Reflections* (San Francisco: Harper Torchbooks, 1970), 14–16 and passim.

14. On this secondary public that "overhears," see William C. Placher, *Narratives of a Vulnerable God: Christ, Theology, and Scripture* (Louisville, Ky.: Westminster John Knox Press, 1994).

15. Ellen F. Davis, "And Pharaoh Will Change His Mind . . .," SBLSP, 1993, proposes that in Ezekiel 32:31 Pharaoh repents and submits to Yahweh. Her rendering is at variance with the conventional consensus but warrants careful consideration.

16. More generally on this perspective, see the fine statement by William H. Willimon, *Peculiar Speech: Preaching to the Baptized* (Grand Rapids: Wm. B. Eerdmans Publishing Co., 1992).

Chapter 5.
Rhetoric and Community

1. James Muilenburg, "Form Criticism and Beyond," *JBL* 88 (1969): 1–18.
2. On the difficult and important distinction between literalism and historicity, see Gerard Loughlin, "Using Scripture: Community and Letterality," in *Words Remembered, Texts Renewed: Essays in Honour of John F. A. Sawyer*, ed. John Davies et al. (JSOTSup 195; Sheffield: Sheffield Academic Press, 1995), 321–39.
3. Ricoeur's work is multifaceted and scattered in many places. For a direct discussion of biblical interpretation, see Paul Ricoeur, *Essays on Biblical Interpretation* (Philadelphia: Fortress Press, 1980). For a splendid essay introducing his work, see Mark I. Wallace, "Introduction," in Paul Ricoeur, *Figuring the Sacred: Religion, Narrative, and Imagination* (Minneapolis: Fortress Press, 1995), 1–32.
4. Among Ricoeur's many discussions of imagination, see "The Bible and Imagination," ibid., 144–66. See also Richard Kearney, *The Wake of Imagination: Toward a Postmodern Culture* (Minneapolis: University of Minnesota Press, 1988).
5. Among his many writings on the subject, see Paul Ricoeur, "World of the Text, World of the Reader," in *A Ricoeur Reader: Reflection and Imagination*, ed. Mario J. Valdes (Toronto: University of Toronto Press, 1991), 491–97. See also Amos N. Wilder, "Story and Story-World," *Interpretation* 37 (1983): 353–64.
6. Paul Ricoeur, "Biblical Hermeneutics," *Semeia* 4 (1975): 31, 127, and passim.
7. Jacob Neusner, *The Enchantments of Judaism: Rites of Transformation from Birth through Death* (New York: Basic Books, 1987), especially pp. 211–16.
8. Phyllis Trible, *God and the Rhetoric of Sexuality* (OBT; Philadelphia: Fortress Press, 1987); *Texts of Terror: Literary-Feminist Readings of Biblical Narratives* (OBT; Philadelphia: Fortress Press, 1984); and *Rhetorical Criticism: Context, Method, and the Book of Jonah* (GBS; Minneapolis: Fortress Press, 1994).
9. On the relation between "what" and "how," see Gail R. O'Day, *The Word Disclosed: John's Story and Narrative Preaching* (St. Louis: CBP Press, 1987).
10. I use the phrase "limit adverbs" with deliberate reference to Paul Ricoeur, "Biblical Hermeneutics," 107–44, and his notion of "limit experiences" and "limit expressions."
11. On this text, see my previous discussion, Walter Brueggemann, "The Embarrassing Footnote," *Theology Today* 44 (1987): 5–14.
12. My intention here closely parallels that of the fine statement of William H. Willimon, *Peculiar Speech: Preaching to the Baptized* (Grand Rapids: Wm. B. Eerdmans Publishing Co., 1992).
13. On the strategy of Elisha and the Pauline mandate, see Walter Wink, "Jesus' Third Way: Nonviolent Engagement," in *Engaging the Powers: Discernment*

and Resistance in a World of Domination (Minneapolis: Fortress Press, 1992), 175–93.

14. Gilbert Ryle, *Collected Papers II*, cited by Clifford Geertz, "Thick Description: Toward an Interpretive Theory of Cultures," in *The Interpretation of Cultures: Selected Essays* (New York: Basic Books, 1973), 6.

15. Ibid., 3–30.

16. Michael Walzer, *Thick and Thin: Moral Argument at Home and Abroad* (Notre Dame, Ind.: University of Notre Dame Press, 1994), xi.

17. For the standard reference to this approach, see Michael Fishbane, *Biblical Interpretation in Ancient Israel* (Oxford: Clarendon Press, 1985).

18. See Richard B. Hays, *Echoes of Scripture in the Letters of Paul* (New Haven, Conn.: Yale University Press, 1989), for a study of the use of such allusions.

19. My argument is much informed by George A. Lindbeck, *The Nature of Doctrine: Religion and Theology in a Postliberal Age* (Philadelphia: Westminster Press, 1984), who takes "experiential-expressive" models of theology as his primary target.

20. The phrase is from Martin Buber, *Moses* (Atlantic Highlands, N.J.: Humanities Press International, 1946), 75–76, who uses the choice phrase to characterize "miracle." More broadly, see Walter Brueggemann, *Abiding Astonishment: Psalms, Modernity, and the Making of History* (Literary Currents in Biblical Interpretation; Louisville, Ky.: Westminster/John Knox Press, 1991).

21. Jack Miles, *God: A Biography* (New York: Alfred A. Knopf, 1995).

22. I refer to "coded winks," following Geertz, "Thick Description," 6–7, who reflects on the social freight carried by a wink in a community that knows the code.

Chapter 6.
Overhearing the Good News

1. The struggle to maintain a distinctive theological identity in a hostile or indifferent environment is of course not new for Jews, as it is for Christians in the West. Taken historically, the matter is not symmetrical for the two communities. It is my point, nonetheless, that the issue before the two communities is now in a very rough way parallel, because of the wholesale disestablishment of Christianity in the West. It has not been parallel in times past, during Christian domination of the West, which included marginalization of Judaism.

2. Charles Reich, *Opposing the System* (New York: Random House, 1995).

3. On the global domination of free market ideology, see Theodore H. von Laue, *The World Revolution of Westernization: The Twentieth Century in Global Perspective* (Oxford: Oxford University Press, 1987), and more ideologically, Francis Fukuyama, *The End of History and the Last Man* (New York: Free Press, 1992).

4. On the one hand, David Tracy, *The Analogical Imagination: Christian Theology and the Culture of Pluralism* (New York: Crossroad, 1981), is the boldest of a "universal," that is, nonchurch hermeneutic. He insists that the theological claims of the faith do not privilege the church, but that there are always "three

publics" with which the theological claims are concerned: the *church* (to be sure), but also the *academy* and *society*. The important insistence of Tracy is that teaching, preaching, and interpretation cannot be confined to or exclusively shaped for a church consitutency, for the claims of faith pertain to public issues. This is an exceedingly important insistence that must concern every preacher.

It is fair to say, however, that Tracy's programmatic vision makes a number of people nervous (including me), for the practice of theology as "public discourse" seems very often to move from assumptions and premises that are profoundly compromised, either in terms of epistemological presuppositions or more blatantly, in accommodation to the socioeconomic hegemony of the day. Most scandalously, much so-called public theology (as in the work of Richard Neuhaus, Michael Novak, and Peter Berger) turns out to be such an accommodation to established hegemony that it is not much more than a blatant neoconservatism that defends free market ideology and tends to equate it with Christian faith. Such an accommodation, to be sure, is not what Tracy has in mind nor would he agree with such a construal of public theology. Nonetheless, one wonders about any such universalism, whether it must in principle compromise the sharp-edged central claims of biblical faith that are rooted in theology but articulated in socioeconomic practices and policies of justice.

The alternative view of theological interpretation to that of Tracy aims first of all at the reality of the church, and has been given its definitive statement by George Lindbeck (*The Nature of Doctrine: Religion and Theology in a Postliberal Age* [Philadelphia: Westminster Press, 1984]). Lindbeck's influential statement urged that the claims of Christian teaching and the credibility of Christian rhetoric must be determined by attentiveness to the church's own "rules of grammar," without reference to any external judgment. Stanley Hauerwas and William Willimon (*Resident Aliens: A Provocative Christian Assessment of Culture and Ministry for People Who Know That Something Is Wrong* [Nashville: Abingdon Press, 1989]), have pressed the particular ecclesial implication to insist that Christians are "resident aliens" and that distinctive identity for Christians in the world is what matters to the theological enterprise. See also Stanley Hauerwas, *After Christiendom? How the Church Is to Behave If Freedom, Justice, and a Christian Nature Are Bad Ideas* (Nashville: Abingdon Press, 1991). It will be readily seen that this position is reflected in what I have said in chapters 4 and 5 in this study, and that I am deeply influenced by and indebted to this posture.

The gains of this "postliberal" position are important. It invites a radical articulation of faith in the "peculiar speech" of the church, that is, the speech of the trusted faith tradition, without having to accommodate to the "canon of reason" that is operative, either in the Enlightenment academy or in the common incidental discourse of "the public," which are driven by commitments other than those of the faith. See William H. Willimon, *Peculiar Speech: Preaching to the Baptized* (Grand Rapids: Wm. B. Eerdmans Publishing Co., 1992). It is important to acknowledge that Hauerwas and Willimon have not excluded "the nonbaptized" in their focus on the baptized. See William H. Willimon, *The Intrusive Word: Preaching to the Unbaptized* (Grand Rapids: Wm. B. Eerdmans Publishing Co., 1994), and William H. Willimon and Stanley Hauerwas, *Preaching to Strangers: Evangelism in Today's World* (Louisville, Ky.: Westminster/John Knox Press, 1992). The intention of this way of thinking about theology and preaching is to liberate the church from censors of cultural expectation, in order that the church can be its own true self in the world. It is difficult to overstate the urgency of this point in our current context of preaching.

At the same time, the criticisms of this "postliberal" position are not difficult to anticipate. On the one hand, if the church talks only to itself without attending to the credibility of its claims beyond the church, it effectively retreats from the world and is unable to speak effectively in "the public square." Indeed, James Gustafson ("The Sectarian Temptation: Reflections on Theology, the Church and the University," *Proceedings of the Catholic Theological Society* 40 [1988]: 83–94) has dismissed such an enterprise as "sectarian" and of course those criticized are not unaware of the criticism. See Lindbeck, "The Sectarian Future of the Church," in *The God Experience: Essays in Hope*, ed. Joseph P. Whelen S.J. (New York: Newman Press, 1971), 226–43, and Walter Brueggemann, "The Legitimacy of a Sectarian Hermeneutic: 2 Kings 18–19," in *Interpretation and Obedience: From Faithful Reading to Faithful Living* (Minneapolis: Fortress Press, 1991), 41–69.

On the other hand, Hauerwas is shrewdly critiqued by Gloria Albrecht (*The Character of Our Communities: Toward an Ethic of Liberation for the Church* [Nashville: Abingdon Press, 1995]) precisely for "universalizing" his particular perspective.

5. The discussion, of course, cannot be reduced to exchanges between Tracy and Lindbeck, though particular attention should be paid to Tracy's appreciative discussion of the work of Lindbeck—David Tracy, "On Reading the Scriptures Theologically," in *Theology and Dialogue: Essays in Conversation with George Lindbeck*, ed. Bruce D. Marshall (Notre Dame, Ind.: University of Notre Dame Press, 1990), 35–68. Tracy's discussion includes a bibliography of the ongoing exchange. See also Stuart Kendall, "Intratextual Theology in a Postmodern World," in *Postmodern Theologies: The Challenge of Religious Diversity*, ed. John Edwards et al. (Maryknoll, N.Y.: Orbis Books, 1995), 91–113. Attention should especially be paid to the work of Hans Frei, particularly *The Eclipse of Biblical Narrative: A Study in Eighteenth and Nineteenth Century Hermeneutics* (New Haven, Conn.: Yale University Press, 1974). For a critical assessment of Frei's work in relation to preaching, see Charles Lamar Campbell, "Preaching Jesus: Hans Frei's Theology and the Contours of a Postliberal Homiletic" (Ph.D. diss., Duke University, 1993).

6. William Placher, *Narratives of a Vulnerable God: Christ, Theology, and Scripture* (Louisville, Ky.: Westminster John Knox Press, 1994). See also Placher, *Unapologetic Theology: A Christian Voice in a Pluralistic Conversation* (Louisville, Ky.: Westminster/John Knox Press, 1989).

7. On the theme of "overhearing," see the use made of Søren Kierkegaard's notion by Fred B. Craddock, *Overhearing the Gospel* (Nashville: Abingdon Press, 1978). Less directly, see Gerald T. Sheppard, "'Enemies' and the Politics of Prayer in the Book of Psalms," in *The Bible and the Politics of Exegesis*, ed. David Jobling et al. (Cleveland: Pilgrim Press, 1991), 61–82.

8. Douglas John Hall, "Ecclesia Crisis: The Theologic of Christian Awkwardness," in *The Church Between Gospel and Culture: The Emerging Mission in North America*, ed. George R. Hunsberger and Craig Von Gelder (Grand Rapids: Wm. B. Eerdmans Publishing Co., 1996), 198–213.

9. See Walter Brueggemann, *Israel's Praise: Doxology against Idolatry and Ideology* (Philadelphia: Fortress Press, 1988), 78–80 and passim.

10. The "dense code" appeals to Lindbeck's "rules of grammar," which in turn are derived from the "thick description" of Clifford Geertz and Gilbert Ryle.

11. I have had it happen occasionally in teaching in front of cameras, that the camera operators become genuinely interested in what is being said, even when it is said in the coded cadences of baptism.

12. Walter Brueggemann, *Biblical Perspectives on Evangelism: Living in a Three-Storied Universe* (Nashville: Abingdon Press, 1993), 26–30 and passim.

13. This translation that reflects cultic immediacy is suggested by Sigmund Mowinckel in his magisterial hypothesis on the Enthronement Psalms. For a review of the problem, see Ben C. Ollenburger, *Zion the City of the Great King: A Theological Symbol of the Jerusalem Cult* (JSOTSup 41; Sheffield: Sheffield Academic Press, 1987), 28–33.

14. The question has become a rather moot one in current scholarship. For reviews of the issue, see the older discussions of A. R. Johnson, "The Psalms," in *The Old Testament and Modern Study: A Generation of Discovery and Research*, ed. H. H. Rowley (Oxford: Clarendon Press, 1951), 190–97; Hans-Joachim Kraus, *Die Koenigsherrschaft Gottes im Alten Testament: Untersuchungen zu den Liedern von Jahwes Thronbesteigung* (Tübingen: J.C.B. Mohr, 1951); and Kraus, *Worship in Israel: A Cultic History of the Old Testament* (Richmond: John Knox Press, 1966), 203–22.

15. The texts most often included in this genre are Isaiah 13—23; Jeremiah 46—51; Ezekiel 25—32; Amos 1:3–23; Obadiah; Nahum; Zephaniah 2:4–15. Among the more helpful discussions, see John H. Hayes, "The Usage of Oracles against Foreign Nations in Ancient Israel," *JBL* 87 (1968): 81–92; Herbert Donner, *Israel Unter den Volkern: Die Stellung der klassischen Propheten des 8 Jahrkunderts V. Chr. zur Aussenpolitik der Könige von Israel und Juda* (*VTSup* 11; Leiden: E. J. Brill, 1964); and Norman K. Gottwald, *All the Kingdoms of the Earth: Israelite Prophecy and International Relations in the Ancient Near East* (New York: Harper & Row, 1964).

16. Paul Raabe, "Why Prophetic Oracles against the Nations?" in *Fortunate the Eyes That See: Essays in Honor of David Noel Freedman*, ed. Astrid B. Beck et al. (Grand Rapids: Wm. B. Eerdmans Publishing Co., 1995), 236–57. Raabe proposes a parallel between these ancient prophets and contemporary religious advocates:

> One can perhaps find an analogy in the practice of contemporary preachers who address governmental officials and proclaim ideal government policies, even though no government official happens to be present in the audience. Preachers intend by such sermons to make a serious statement of how from their perspective the government should behave and of what policies it ought to

follow. If interviewed, these preachers would express hope that the government would heed this counsel and change for the better (248).

17. Ibid., 252.
18. To that extent, I believe that a "canonical" approach is more helpful than any historical reconstruction, for the oracles have their function now within the literary contexts of the prophetic books. Brevard S. Childs, *Introduction to the Old Testament as Scripture* (Philadelphia: Fortress Press, 1979), 352–53, 401–403, has made some passing references to the canonical function of these oracles, but the question remains to be studied in depth.
19. It can be plausibly argued, for example, that in the "final form" of the Exodus narrative (Exodus 1—15), the central point is not the rescue of Israel, but the glorification of Yahweh in the eyes of the nations.
20. While the praxis of Yahweh seems a strange notion midst the cognitive approaches of historical criticism, it seems evident that these oracles were concerned for the *practice* and not the *naming* of Yahweh. The most acute text concerning the "doing of Yahweh" is Jeremiah 22:15–26, on which see José Miranda, *Marx and the Bible: Critique of the Philosophy of Oppression* (Maryknoll, N.Y.: Orbis Books, 1974), 46–72.
21. Donald Gowan, *When Man Becomes God: Humanism and Hubris in the Old Testament* (Pittsburgh: Pickwick Press, 1975), has considered texts in which foreign powers act in prideful autonomy and inevitably become exploitative and brutalizing.
22. On the notion of Yahweh as the administrator of a realm over which Yahweh has rights and responsibilities for governance, see G. Ernest Wright, "The Nations in Hebrew Prophecy," *Encounter* 26 (Winter 1965): 225–37, and George E. Mendenhall, "The Vengeance of Yahweh," in *The Tenth Generation: The Origins of the Biblical Tradition* (Baltimore: Johns Hopkins University Press, 1973), 69–104. John Barton, *Amos's Oracles Against the Nations: A Study of Amos 1:3–2:5* (Cambridge: Cambridge University Press, 1980), has suggested that the "sanctions" given in these oracles against the nations do not need to be understood in a supernaturalist way, but are the ordinary happenings in the life of geopolitics. I have suggested that the more "naturalistic" sanctions of Paul M. Kennedy, *The Rise and Fall of the Great Powers: Economic Change and Military Conflict from 1500–2000* (New York: Random House, 1987), may be a useful way to understand what is being asserted in these oracles.
23. See Raabe, "Why Prophetic Oracles," 244–47.
24. See particularly Walter Wink, *Engaging the Powers: Discernment and Resistance in a World of Domination* (Minneapolis: Fortress Press, 1992), and Ched Myers, *Binding the Strong Man: A Political Reading of Mark's Story of Jesus* (Maryknoll, N.Y.: Orbis Books, 1990).
25. On the large horizon of faith in which Israel is set in context in the Old Testament, see Patrick D. Miller, "Creation and Covenant," in *Biblical Theology: Problems and Perspectives*, ed. Steven J. Kraftchick et al. (Nashville: Abingdon Press, 1995), 155–68. See also Walter Brueggemann, "The Transformative Potential of a Public Metaphor: Isaiah 37:21–29," in *Interpretation and Obedi-*

ence, 70–99. The recovery of this horizon of biblical faith is urgent in the concrete discourse of the congregation, a horizon almost completely forfeited in the privatizing propensities of the Enlightenment.

26. On the great theological weight carried by the Jerusalem temple and site, see Ben C. Ollenberger, *Zion the City of the Great King*.

27. In addition to Ollenburger, see Hartmut Gese, *Essays on Biblical Theology* (Minneapolis: Augsburg Publishing House, 1981), 79–85, who suggests that Zion becomes the locus of Torah rather than Sinai; Norman K. Gottwald, *All the Kingdoms of the Earth*, 199–203, who proposes that "a machinery of adjudication" is put in place in this vision of Jerusalem that resituates Israel as one among many peoples over whom Yahweh exercises governance.

28. See Walter Brueggemann, "Vine and Fig Tree: A Case Study in Imagination and Criticism," *CBQ* 43 (1981): 188–204.

29. Ollenburger, *Zion the City of the Great King*, 159, for the high claims he makes on the theological claims of Zion, must concede that in practice ("on historical grounds"), matters appear to have been different, as the royal-temple establishment was not immune to the seductions of ideological power.

30. See Walter Brueggemann, "Pharaoh as Vassal: A Study of a Political Metaphor," *CBQ* 57 (1995): 27–51.

31. On this text, see Walter Brueggemann, "Subversive Modes of Blessing," (forthcoming).

32. For a current assessment of the old "Midianite hypothesis" of the origins of Yahwism, see Moshe Weinfeld, "The Tribal League at Sinai," in *Ancient Israelite Religion: Essays in Honor of Frank Moore Cross*, ed. Patrick D. Miller et al. (Philadelphia: Fortress Press, 1987), 303–14. In any case, such questions as the origins of Yahwism lie outside the scope of this study and outside the interpretive perspective urged here.

33. Here I assume a "class reading" of the text and assume something like the hypothesis of a "peasant revolt" that Rahab apparently aided and abetted.

Chapter 7.
Rethinking Church Models through Scripture

1. Avery Dulles, *Models of the Church* (Garden City, N.Y.: Doubleday & Co., 1974); Paul S. Minear, *Images of the Church in the New Testament* (Philadelphia: Westminster Press, 1960).

2. H. Richard Niebuhr, *Christ and Culture* (New York: Harper & Brothers, 1951).

3. It is not remote from my argument that an analogue exists between the royal-temple establishment in ancient Israel and the Constantinian establishment of the church. Thus the "end of the Constantinian period" in the church is congenial to my argument.

4. For one possible rendering of the social function of the sages, see George E. Mendenhall, "The Study Side of Wisdom: The Date and Purpose of Genesis 3," in *A Light Unto My Path*, ed. Howard N. Bream et al. (Philadelphia: Temple University Press, 1974), 319–34.

5. See J. David Pleins, "Poverty in the Social World of the Wise," *JSOT* 37 (1987): 61–78.

6. This argument is made with greatest clarity and passion in the traditions of Jeremiah and Ezekiel.

7. Such a juxtaposition of Leviticus and Deuteronomy is shrewdly rendered by Fernando Belo, *A Materialist Reading of the Gospel of Mark* (Maryknoll, N.Y.: Orbis Books, 1981), 1–86 and passim.

8. George Lindbeck, "The Church," in *Keeping the Faith: Essays to Mark the Centenary of Lux Munde*, ed. Geoffrey Wainwright (Philadelphia: Fortress Press, 1988), 179–208, has argued that "storied community" is the primary identifying mark of Christian ecclesiology.

9. I deliberately use the phrasing of George A. Lindbeck, *The Nature of Doctrine: Religion and Theology in a Postliberal Age* (Philadelphia: Westminster Press, 1984). I believe that the categories of Lindbeck's argument greatly illuminate the practice of ancient Israel when it lacked cultural institutions of support.

10. Daniel L. Smith, *The Religion of the Landless: The Social Context of the Babylonian Exile* (Bloomington, Ind.: Meyer-Stone Books, 1989).

11. "Notes and Comments," *The New Yorker* (May 21, 1990): 27–28.

12. I have found the ideas of Stephen Toulmin's *Cosmopolis: The Hidden Agenda of Modernity* (New York: Free Press, 1990) most helpful, but there is a growing literature on the subject.

Scripture Index